THE PRINCE OF URBAN LITERATURE

Eric B Crime Novels, LLC

Note: This book is a work of fiction. Names, characters, places and incidents are products of the author's imagination or are used fictitiously. Any resemblance to actual events, locale, or persons living or dead, is entirely coincidental.

Published by: Eric B Crime Novels, LLC

Eric B Crime Novels, LLC
P.O Box 345
Wilmington, DE 19899

Copyright date: 2012
ISBN: 978-1-944151-24-9

As Dirty As It Gets Story by Wasiim

Edited by: Navimjan Services LLC
Cover design by: Vultran Creative, www.vultran.net
Formatted by: Krystol Diggs
Typed from handwriting to text by: Vanessa Cooper
Female model on cover: Janiqua Drumgold, janiquad18@gmail.com
Male models: Pretty Thugger and Danger

All Eric B Crime Novel titles are available at special quantity discounts for bulk purchases for sales promotion, fund-raising, educational, or institutional use and book clubs.

www.streetknowledgepublishing.com

Printed in Canada

A Note From the Author

Although this is a work of fiction I want it to be noted that these things can really happen. The decisions YOU make can affect your family, friends and everyone else you may be around. The streets have no heart and bullets have no names. Yes, I want you to be entertained by my work, but please also take a deeper understanding of the things that take place in this novel. Examine each character, the decisions that they make, and watch how the consequences unfold. Don't let it happen to you.

Thank you for your support. I hope you enjoy the book. Please email me at loyaltyinkpublishing@gmail.com for any feedback you'd like to give. Also I'm available on Facebook: http://www.facebook.com/wasiim.young.

Thank You,

Kenneth Young
a.k.a.
Wasiim

Acknowledgements

First and foremost I want to thank Allah for giving me the talent, skill and patience I needed to complete another book. I thank Him for everyone who has supported me and read my work. I would also like to thank Him for allowing me to humble myself so that I could learn more about writing and become a better author. Ameen.

Shout outs for this book will be real short. If you feel as though you deserved a shout out and didn't get one I'm sorry about that. It's nothing personal. This is just the most difficult part of the book. Lol. You know I love you!

To my daughters, Amoni and London Young, I want y'all to know that you two are the reason I breathe. I love y'all with all my heart and soul. Nothing on this earth will ever come before y'all. I'm sorry for the poor choices that I made that cost us so much time apart. I know I'll never be able to make up for that lost time but know that I will forever strive to be the best father I can be. I love y'all.

I want to thank my Mom, Quita Blackstock, for birthing me and raising me to be a good man. I thank you for all the life lessons you've taught me over the years and I want you to know that I was listening to you even though I didn't always do as you said! Lol. Love you.

I want to give my Dad, Michael Blackstock, a special thank you. I want to thank you for raising me as if I was your own for as long as I can remember. I thank you for teaching me what a real man is and being an example of one. You're a special man and I'm glad Allah has placed you in my life. I couldn't have asked for a better father. Love you.

To my family, it's too many of y'all to name individually but I love you all. I thank y'all for all the support y'all have showed me. And that's to all my aunts, uncles and cousins on all sides of my family.

Janae and Aunt Lisa, I know y'all lost Steph, but I want y'all to know that y'all will always have a son and brother in me. I'm here for y'all, never forget that. I love y'all.

Bria Blackstock, my baby sis, I love you and I want you to know that I'll always be there for you. You can come to me for anything. I want you to stay focused and become a successful woman. I love you.

Shout out to Quiet Loyalty Empire. My brother Kendell. Love you bro. And my homie Vel. We on that mission and we'll reach every goal we set, Insha Allah. Prayer, focus and determination.

Yo, I always got to shout out my three homies that been with me that longest. Ty, Eric, and Danny, love y'all like brothers. Real talk.

To the mothers of my two Princesses, Kina Smith and Celita Maddrey, I want y'all to know that I appreciate how y'all hold my daughters down. I apologize for forcing y'all to do it on y'all own while I was away. I wish y'all nothing but happiness and peace. Insha Allah we'll always remain friends.

I would like thank my Editor, Muhammad Al-Mahdi, for taking the time to not only edit my work, but for teaching me how to craft my skill as well. I thank you for all the books on writing you've given me and for actually letting me know I needed to sharpen up. With your help I was able to take my writing to another level and I thank you for that.

To my readers, I thank y'all for y'all's patience. I know y'all been cussing me out for taking so long to put these books out. I promise this book will be worth the wait. I will strive for consistency and will be pushing to put out a book at least once a year. I need y'all help to succeed so don't forget to post those reviews on amazon.com and any other place you can put a review. Oh yeah, remember to LIKE my books on Amazon. That helps more than y'all may know. Also feel free to email me. I'll return your emails.

loyaltyinkpublishing@gmail.com.

I want to thank a few of my fellow authors who were kind enough to help me. Krystol Diggs, Quiana Johnson, Tammy Capri, Jade Jones, Al Saddiq Banks, and especially K.D Harris, she's one of the realist people I ever met in my life! And I'd like to thank L.Prince a.k.a Lee Mudd the author of the BLOODY MONEY series for leading the way for all of the Delaware authors. Also I want y'all to look out for the future authors that will be with Loyalty Ink Publishing, James Freeman, Tariq Ford and Jawanna Booker.

To all my homies that are locked up right now, keep your head up and never give up. Know that it's a better way than the streets. Take the time you have on the inside and READ. Read self-help books and books that teach you how to really get money. The streets ain't it anymore. Got to switch up.

Stephfon Phillips a.k.a Catman, you may be gone but will never be forgotten. I love you bro. Insha Allah you reach paradise. Ripper, Magic, Newz, Q-ball, Sparks, G-Money, Keese, Lil Wells, Rama dan, Star, sorry if I missed anyone. Too many falling soldiers to re-member, but all of y'all know that y'all aren't forgotten.

This book is dedicated to my Mom and
Dad
Quita and Michael Blackstock

I love Y'all

chapter one

"This movie better be good," Esco said with a smile when he looked over at Sinnamon from the driver's seat of the Bentley.

"And what are you going to do if it isn't?" Sinnamon asked. "You plan to rough me up?"

Esco allowed his eyes to roam down to the swell of Sinnamon's breast then to her thick thighs. He licked his lips. "We can skip the movie and get straight to the rough shit. The tint is dark enough. Where you want me to park?"

"Boy, you are so nasty."

"You started it, but I can wait 'til the movie's—" Esco cell phone rang.

Sinnamon grabbed the phone from the cup holder then handed it to him. He looked at the phone's small screen. A smile spread across his face when he saw Flip's name. He answered, "What's good cousin?"

"I don't know what's good no more, Es," Flip said. "Shit's crazy, that's why I'm calling you."

There was a slight edge in Flip's voice. Esco pushed a button on the steering wheel and the car's stereo system shut down.

"You alright, dawg?" Esco asked. "You ain't got no problems do you?"

"That bitch you with my problem. Please tell me that ain't ya girl, Es."

"Bitch? What bitch you talking about?"

"The one you just picked up from the projects."

As Dirty As It Gets

Esco pulled the phone away from his ear and stared at it. Flip must've lost his mind. "Hold up, cousin, don't ever call me disrespecting my fucking wife. Nigga, you crazy? I don't know what's good, but I'ma take it as you ain't know who she was."

"Damn, Es, I was hoping you ain't say nothing like that." Flip paused for a moment. "That's one of the bitches that robbed and shot me."

Esco looked over at Sinnamon. He couldn't believe what Flip said. What was Sinnamon doing robbing people? Flip's unreasonable ass at that. He quickly pulled into the parking lot of the Citgo gas station on Concord Avenue. A small crowd of young boys stood in front of the store. Esco pulled in front of them before continuing his conversation.

"What the fuck is you talking about?" Esco said. He looked over at Sinnamon again and still couldn't believe the world was so small.

"Nigga, stop playing, you know what the fuck I'm talking about. You sent her and her friend down ATL to handle me. Why me though, dawg?"

"You know I ain't have nothing to do—"

"You ain't have nothing to do with it?" Flip said, then chuckled. "So what I'm supposed to think...it was all some big coincidence? I was wondering why Mills was so pressed to let shit ride. You niggas is foul. Gonna set me up though?"

"Ain't nobody set you up. Set you up for what?"

"Whatever, I got something for you niggas though. You muthafuckas think shit's a game, but I ain't playing. Tell that bitch you with I already killed her girl and the bitch she just dropped her son off to. I'ma kill her next."

"Aye yo, Flip, I swear to fucking God, you touch her I'ma kill you."

"Kill me and y'all won't ever see her son again."

"Flip, Flip," Esco yelled into his cell phone, but Flip didn't respond. When he realized Flip had hung up, he banged his fist against the steering wheel repeatedly. His options were limited with Shaquan in the mix of things. It was best he relax and try a more humble approach. He dialed Flip's number and prayed he picked up.

"Got ya attention now, huh?" Flip said.

"Flip," Esco said as calmly as he could.

"Esco," Flip replied.

"That little boy ain't got nothing to do with this."

"I ain't say he did, but we at war. I'ma use everything to my advantage. You mutha-fuckas should've thought about that little nigga before y'all decided to pull that stunt."

"How many times I gotta tell you I ain't have shit to do with it. She ain't know who you was, dawg."

"I'm sorry, Es, but I can't believe that. I'ma think about the little boy and see what I want to do. For the right price I might let him go. Until then, don't worry. He'll be in good hands. I won't let nothing bad happen to him as long as you don't get out of line."

Flip disconnected the call.

Esco threw his phone down on his lap. He banged both of his fists against the steering wheel again then rested his forehead against it. He rubbed his fingers through the back of his braids. Tears of frustration streamed down his face. He never felt so helpless.

Sinnamon reached over from the passenger seat and rubbed his back.

He pushed her away from him. "Don't fucking touch me."

"What did I do?"

He lifted his head and stared at her. How could she look so damn innocent when she was running around robbing and shooting people?

"You robbed the wrong nigga," he said.

"What are you talking about?" She really looked confused and that pissed him off even more.

"That shit y'all did in Atlanta. That was a nigga I was cool with. He was up here visiting. I was supposed to introduce you to him yesterday, but he must've seen you already."

For a split second Sinnamon's eyes grew wide. "I don't know who you're talking about," she said.

"Sinnamon, that nigga Flip ain't die. He's up here. He said he killed Essence and Ms. Jones."

"What do you mean?"

"What I mean?" Esco let out a chuckle. "I mean that little bull-shit y'all thought was cute, running around robbing niggas and shit, got ya girl and Ms. Jones murdered. Them mutha-fuckas took Shaquan too."

"What are you talking about? Who took my brother?"

"They kidnapped him."

"Who the fuck is they, Esco?" Sinnamon sobbed. "Who the fuck is they." She swung her small fist in Esco's direction.

Esco grabbed a hold of her wrist then pulled her to him. He hugged her tight as she cried a river of tears.

"Who has my brother?" Sinnamon sobbed into Esco's chest.

He rocked her back and forth, trying to calm her down. "Don't worry we gonna get him back." He held her a while longer then said, "Come on, baby, we gotta go check on Ms. Jones and Essence."

chapter two

When Esco rode into the projects everything seemed normal. The neighborhood was swarming with people, mainly drug dealers and their loyal customers. Despite the time of night and the chill in the air, small children ran freely throughout the neighborhood.

Esco slowed down as he approached Ms. Jones's place then made a complete stop in front of Sinnamon's old home. The only light coming from Sinnamon's was the flickering of the TV in the living room. Next door at Ms. Jones's, a dim light shined through the windows. Nothing seemed out of place, but Esco knew death was in the air.

He fiddled with a few buttons on the dashboard. The driver's seat hummed then clicked. He reached under the seat and pulled out a nickel-plated 9mm from the stash spot he'd activated. He cocked the gun back loading a hollow-tipped bullet into the chamber. With the gun clutched tight in his hand he looked over at Sinnamon.

"Stay in the car," he said, opening the driver's door.

Sinnamon totally ignored what Esco told her and was out the car before he stepped two feet away. He wanted to order her back in, but knew that would lead to an argument and now wasn't the time for that.

When they got in front of the house, Esco noticed the door was ajar. A closer inspection revealed that the door jamb was splintered and cracked. He pushed the door open with his foot then entered with his gun pointed. Sinnamon kept close behind him, gripping the back of his shirt as they walked.

Esco spotted Essence lying lifelessly on the couch, blood trick-

As Dirty As It Gets

ling from a small hole in her forehead; more blood covering her shirt and soaking the couch. He stopped in his tracks and Sinnamon ran into his back. She turned on the light then peeked around him. She screamed.

"Oh my God, Essence!" Sinnamon rushed over to her best friend. She kneeled beside her and shook her violently. "Essence get up! Please get up!"

"Come on, baby, she's gone," Esco said softly. He tried to pull Sinnamon away from the body but she jerked away from him.

"I don't want to leave her." She looked up at Esco with a tear stained face that broke his heart. He decided to give her some time alone with her friend and went to check on Ms. Jones.

When he entered Ms. Jones's, he could tell a struggle had taken place. Ms. Jones's normally tidy living room looked like a tornado hit it. The couch was turned over, and shattered dishes along with broken pictures were all over the floor. Esco found her with a single gunshot wound on the right side of her nose. She was lying with her arms stretched outward as if she was reaching for something. Esco shook his head at the sight. He thought on how good of a woman Ms. Jones was and felt she didn't deserve to die like that. Flip was taking things too far and needed to be stopped. Once he got Shaquan back Esco planned to do just that.

"Come the fuck on little nigga," Bone said. He grabbed Shaquan by his shirt and attempted to drag him out of the car.

"No! I wanna go home!" Shaquan yelled through his tears. He gripped onto the back of the passenger seat for dear life and kicked his little feet like a raging bull, barley missing Bone's face.

Bone punched Shaquan in his gut. The little boy released the strong hold he had on the seat and clutched his stomach. Bone yanked him out of the car, threw him over this shoulder then made his way to Flip's house.

"This little mutha-fucka kinda strong," Bone said when he entered the front room of the house. He tossed Shaquan on the couch, adjacent to the one Flip and Newz sat, then flopped down beside him.

Flip looked over at Bone. "Lock him in my room."

"I ain't fucking with that little boy no more," Bone said. "One of you niggas better do it."

13

"Fuck it I'll do it." Newz got up, walked over to Shaquan and snatched him by his collar then dragged him up the steps.

"Where the duck tape?" Newz yelled from the top of the steps.

Bone looked at Flip. "What you do with the tape?"

"I probably left it in the basement," Flip said without looking up.

He was still seated on the sofa deep in thought. In one hand he held a bottle of Heineken, in the other was the gun he killed Essence with. He looked down at the heartless piece of steel he gripped in his hand and wondered if there was a way to avoid a war with his friends. The only compromise he could come up with was the surrender of Sinnamon. That was the only way he'd be convinced that Esco and Mills didn't have anything to do with the robbery. If Esco wasn't willing to give her up, he was prepared to kill all of them.

Bone returned from the basement with the tape in his hand. "So what we gonna do with that nigga downstairs?"

"I'ma go holla at him for a minute and see what he knows."

"You want me to come with you?"

"Naw, go get rid of this." He passed Bone his gun, "dump the ones you and Newz had too."

"Alright," Bone said then headed upstairs.

Flip made his way down to the basement. Mills was laid out on the basement floor in the exact spot he left him. He walked over to him and looked down on his old friend. Mills' mouth was heavily duck taped, so were his hands and feet. Flip kneeled down beside him and unwound the tape from around his head.

"So what's it gonna be?" Flip said.

Mills looked up at Flip through swollen eyes. Dry blood was caked up all over his face, and fresh blood oozed from the gashes on his forehead. He was in need of medical attention but wouldn't get so much as a towel to wipe the blood from his face if he didn't say something Flip wanted to hear.

"What the fuck you mean what's it gonna be?" Mills shouted. "You let me go I'ma kill you pussy."

That wasn't even close to what Flip wanted to hear.

"You wanna play tough." Flip pulled out a .45 from his waistband. He gripped the gun by its barrel and raised it above his head. With all the strength he possessed he smacked Mills with the butt of the gun. The contact made a sickening thud and opened a fresh wound on the side of Mills' face.

"Why the fuck you set me up?" Flip asked.

"I told you I ain't have nothing to do with that shit."

"Then why was you so press to squash the beef?"

"I said I'd ride with you on this shit. I just wanted to leave the fucking game alone. I'm tired of this shit, look how it got you acting. You ain't even thinking no more. You know I wouldn't do you dirty."

Flip wanted to believe Mills, but things weren't adding up. "I ain't tryna hear that shit Mills. If y'all ain't have shit to do with it then how the fuck do you explain ya boy Esco knowing the bitches that did that shit?"

"Like I said we ain't have nothing to do with it."

"How about Gage, he know about the slimy shit you and Esco pulled?"

"We ain't do no slimy shit and Gage was locked up. He's done with the streets, leave that nigga be."

"At least you show some type of loyalty," Flip said, "but on some G-shit, I ain't sure about Gage either. I don't trust none of you niggas no more. I'm about to call that nigga and see what's really good."

Flip tucked his gun back in his waistband then pulled his phone from his back pocket. He dialed Gage and waited for an answer. He planned to get to the bottom of things before the night was over. "So what happened?" Detective Johnson asked Sinnamon. She was leaning against the passenger side of her car while he stood in front of her with a pen and pad in his hands. Occasionally he al- lowed his poppy eyes to scan the length of her body. The tight jeans she wore looked as if they would burst at the seams.

"I don't know," Sinnamon said.

Detective Johnson looked from Sinnamon to the crime scene. Police were going in and out the house collecting evidence, proba- bly getting nothing useful. He was on the verge of losing his pa- tience. He turned his attention back to Sinnamon and gave her his,

WASIIM

I don't believe a word you're saying look.

"There's two dead bodies and you don't know what happened?" He placed his hand on her shoulder then said in a gentler tone, "Did the man with you do this?"

"No stupid." Sinnamon batted the detective's hand from her shoulder then glared into his eyes. "You need to find my brother and stop asking me dumb ass questions. I already told the rest of you idiots we didn't have anything to do with this. For the last time, we dropped my brother off then came back not even fifteen minutes later and found them dead." Tears began to fall from her eyes.

"Do you or your boyfriend sell drugs?" Detective Johnson asked, his tone no longer gentle."

Sinnamon shook her head in disgust. "You guys just don't stop do you? I tell you two of my friends are dead and my little brother is missing but you can't do anything but find ways to blame me. This is ridiculous, I don't want to talk anymore." She folded her arms across her chest then looked toward the houses.

"Chuck let me speak to you for a second," Detective Johnson's partner called out from a few feet away.

Detective Johnson left Sinnamon and made his way over to his partner.

"Yeah, what's up?" Johnson said when he reached him.

"It's the girl who had the murder charge dismissed," Detective Burton replied.

"Essence from the case we were working?"

"The one and only."

"No shit? I guess she got what was coming to her after all. You think that was the motive?"

"Could be," Detective Burton said. "I didn't get much out of the guy on the scene. He refused to talk. Only thing he said was that he didn't know what was going on."

Detective Johnson looked back at Sinnamon. "That's basically what I got out of her." He turned back to his partner. "Your guy say anything about the little boy?"

"Not much. It's a shame how these kids get caught in the cross-fire. I think that Ira guy knows more than what he's saying. I can feel it."

"We'll get to the bottom of this," Detective Johnson said sure of himself.

chapter Three

Gage and Arrissa sat in a private room at Christiana Hospital with some of Shantel's family members. Earlier that day Shantel's mother had decided to take Shantel off of the life support system she had been hooked up to. A few hours later the affect of AIDS claimed another life.

"She looked so different," Arrissa whispered to Gage. They were seated off to the side, away from the grieving family who was saying a prayer for Shantel. Arrissa and Gage, being Muslim, didn't participate in the prayer.

"Yeah, I know. I feel so bad for her. Her mother said she asked for a closed casket. She didn't want nobody to remember her looking sick." Gage felt a twinge of guilt for the role he played in Shantel's death.

After she prayed, Shantel's mother broke away from the rest of the family and made her way over to Gage and Arrissa. She placed her hand on Gage's shoulder. "I thank you and Arrissa both for all the support y'all have shown here lately. The funeral will be next week. I'm sure I'll see y'all there. Hakim is with his aunt right now, but I'll drop him off to you guys later on." She stared into Gage's eyes and took a deep breath. "I'm trying with all my strength to forgive you like Shantel has done, but it's hard. Time heals all wounds but for now, I just ask that you take care of my grandson. Raise him right Anthony, please don't be a disappointment."

"I promise to do right by my son."

Mrs. Carter sighed. "I sure hope so." She gave Gage a hard look then walked off and joined the rest of her family.

As Dirty As It Gets

"You ready to leave?" Arrissa asked when Mrs. Carter was out of earshot. "I feel so out of place right now."

"Yeah, come on." Gage got up from his seat, stretched, then he and Arrissa left the room.

On the elevator Gage thought about all the wrong he'd done over the years and couldn't help but wonder how he, out of all people, managed to get all the blessings he'd received. His 56-year prison sentence had been overturned, he had a beautiful wife and his son was healthy despite his mother being infected with HIV. Allah couldn't have been better to him.

When the elevator reached the lobby it's bell rang, bringing Gage out of his thoughts. He and his wife stepped out then headed to the exit. They left the hospital through the revolving doors and were greeted by the night's cold air.

Arrissa walked close to Gage, using him as a shield from the wind. "Our car would be parked all far away," she said.

Allahu Akbar, Allahu Akbar! Gage's cell phone called out. Gage fished the phone from his coat's inside pocket. "As Sa-laamu Alaykum," he answered.

"Wa alaykum as Salaam."

"What's good with you, Flip?" Gage asked, recognizing the voice.

"Nothing much, you busy?"

"Naw, I'm just leaving the hospital. Shantel died." Gage replied as he and Arrissa walked to their car.

"Death must be in the air all around," Flip said.

"Why you say that?" Gage's voice was full of concern.

"Remember them bitches I told you about that robbed and shot me?" Flip pointed his gun at Mills' head.

"Yeah, what about them?"

"I found them. Funny thing though, I seen them chilling with that nigga Esco. So I had to ask myself, how the fuck do some bitches that know Esco manage to come all the way down ATL and hit me up."

"So what, you think Esco had something to do with it? He don't even know where you live."

"Exactly, you think just like me. That nigga don't know where

19

I live at, so that leaves me with no choice but to think Mills helped set me up."

Flip jammed the gun in Mills' battered face.

"Fuck you," Mills spat from the floor.

"Unless you did it of course," Flip added.

"You know I ain't have nothing to do with that nonsense. I don't think Mills or Esco did either. Neither one of them are broke. None of us are. So why do something so stupid?"

"I'ma tell you like I told them. I don't believe that shit." Flip used his shoulder to hold the phone to his ear while he cocked the gun back. Once a bullet was loaded into the chamber he pressed the barrel against Mills' temple. "I'll tell you this though, I think you're in the clear for now, so you safe, but Mills and Esco gotta go. I know they was in on that shit."

"Flip, we better than that."

"That's what I thought." Flip gripped the gun tighter.

"Come on man, we like family. Let me call Mills and Esco so we can get together and talk this out."

"It's too late. Esco made his choice...he gonna ride with that bitch and Mills right here. You can kiss that nigga good-bye."

Flip pulled the trigger.

The bullet entered one side of Mills' head and exploded out of the other. Brain matter and blood sprayed across the basement floor.

Gage stopped his stride when he heard the gunshot. "Flip, what the fuck man. I know you ain't do what I think you did."

"Fuck that nigga," Flip said. "Esco and that bitch next. Like I told you, you in the clear for now. If you wanna keep it that way, I advise you to fall back, cuz I ain't showing no mercy. Nigga's bitches is getting it too since they want to use them to rob niggas. "

Gage began to feel his old ways resurfacing. He felt Flip's threat was aimed at his wife and that didn't sit well with him. The beast he promised himself he would contain bucked hard against its restraints.

You gonna threaten me and mine nigga?" Gage yelled into the phone.

Arrissa grabbed him by the arm.

As Dirty As It Gets

He gave her a menacing scowl and she backed off.

"So you gonna threaten me and my wife? What you think I'ma bitch now cuz I'm deening? I bust heads too nigga. What you think it's a game."

"Naw, nigga, I think its war. You niggas thought it was a game. I'm up 3 bodies; if you don't want to add to that count, stay the fuck out my way."

The phone went dead.

chapter Four

"You're not leaving this house without me." Sinnamon jumped up from the bed, raced past Esco to their bedroom door and blocked his path. "I'm coming with you."

"Nah, you gonna stay here and chill the fuck out for a minute. I told you, I got this shit under control. I'm about to go meet with my peoples so we can come up with a plan to get Shaquan back."

"And I'm coming. That's my brother, and those were my friends," Sinnamon screamed in Esco's face.

"Listen." Esco grabbed Sinnamon roughly by her arms. "I'ma handle this shit. You don't know the type nigga you dealing with. This ain't how it was when you and Essence was doing whatever the fuck y'all was doing. I ain't gonna risk losing you 'cause you running off emotions. Emotions get you killed, Sinnamon."

"I can handle myself." Sinnamon tried to break free from Esco's grasp but failed.

"I ain't saying you can't but—Fuck it, do you trust me?"
Sinnamon didn't respond. She stared into Esco's eyes searching for an answer.

"I said do you trust me?" Esco asked in a more forceful tone.
Sinnamon sighed. "Yeah, I trust you but—"
Esco put his index finger to her lips. "But nothing. Let me handle this alright. I'm ya man, stand behind me. I ain't gonna let nothing happen to you or Shaquan. I promise." He pulled Sinnamon closer and hugged her. "I love you."

"I love you too," Sinnamon said barley above a whisper.

Esco pulled back from her a little bit. "So you gonna let me handle this without ya help?"

As Dirty As It Gets

"Yes," Sinnamon hesitantly replied.

"Alright, I'ma go holla at my niggas, then I'll be back." Esco strode across the room and into his walk-in closet. He came out carrying a black Tec-9 and walked over to Sinnamon. "Keep this next to you. Don't nobody know where we live, but you can never be too safe. Anybody come to the door call me ASAP."

Sinnamon snatched the gun. "Somebody comes to the door I'ma shoot first and ask questions last."

"Alright baby, I'll be back in a few." Esco kissed Sinnamon on her forehead then left the room, leaving her standing in the doorway.

Out front Esco got into a beige 2002 Grand Marquis. After he situated himself in the driver's seat, he activated his stash box then pulled two 9mm handguns from the hidden compartment underneath the seat. Both guns were fully loaded and ready to be fired. He tucked one under his left thigh and the other one he placed on his lap. With thirty-two shots at his disposal Esco felt ready for whatever might come his way.

He pulled up in front of the barbershop and put his car in park. Before stepping out of the Marquis he tucked both guns in his waistband as a precaution. Inside the barbershop his boys Reef, Beefy and Clark were all there waiting on him. Seeing them show up early in the morning on such a short notice showed him a sense of loyalty he greatly appreciated.

"What's up?" Esco said to the three men.

"Same shit, different day," Beefy said from the barber chair he was seated in. "What's good with you, you alright?"

Esco took a seat in a padded waiting chair adjacent to the ones that Reef and Clark sat in. "Shit's fucked up right now," he said. "My girl's brother got kidnapped last night."

"By who?" Clark asked.

"The boy Flip I was fucking with."

"The Philly nigga?" Reef asked.

"Yeah."

"I told you you couldn't trust those niggas," Reef said.

"So how all this happen?" Clark said.

Esco briefly explained to everyone what happened. He could

23

tell they were all surprised to hear what Sinnamon and Essence had been up to.

"Damn, I would've never guessed," Clark said. "I'm with you though."

"We all with you," Beefy said. "How you plan to go about things?"

"Since Flip got Shaquan we gotta play it smart," Esco said. "I don't want nothing to happen to my young boy. I've been thinking about shit all night. Flip's been staying down ATL for a while now but I remember him saying he still got his spot in Philly."

"You know where it's at?" Clark asked.

"Yeah and I'm trying to see if he got my young boy there."

"When you trying make the move?" Reef asked.

"Tonight. I got a white boy coming up from VA with enough guns to hold down a small army. Once I got all that in place we can move out."

"That's all it is then," Beefy said. "Just let us know when you're ready."

Esco stood up, "I'ma do that."

Sinnamon paced back and forth in the bedroom. Her thoughts wouldn't allow her any rest. Every time she closed her eyes visions of Essence's bloody body invaded her mind, slowly eating away at her sanity. Thinking about her brother made things worse. Her nerves were on edge and guilt tore holes in her soul. She felt as if she could have a nervous breakdown at any minute.

"I know this is all my fault," she said out loud to herself. She stopped pacing when she got in front of the mirror that hung over the dresser. She leaned her face closer to it and didn't like what stared back at her. Her normally well-kept hair was all over the place and her eyes were red and puffy from crying all night.

"I need some rest." She ran her hands up over her face then through her hair. "Maybe a drink will help."

She walked over to her bed and picked up the Tec-9 Esco left her. The gun gave her a small sense of comfort. She yearned to fire it into those responsible for her grief but didn't know where to begin the search for her enemies. There was nothing she could do but wait for Esco to keep his word.

As Dirty As It Gets

Carrying the gun in one hand, she made her way down to the first floor then the kitchen. She sat the Tec on the counter next to the sink then opened a cabinet and grabbed the biggest shot glass she could find. Esco kept a small collection of liquors in the cabinet below the sink so she searched it hoping to find the bottle of Patron she saw him bring in a few days ago. As she searched she was surprised to stumble across a large block of cocaine. Esco wasn't supposed to bring drugs in the house. At least that's what they agreed on.

"I'ma cuss his ass out." She pushed the kilo to the side and found the bottle of Patron behind it. She pulled the bottle out and filled her glass to the brim. She carefully brought the glass to her lips and downed the liquor in one gulp.

"Damn this shit is strong," she said, patting her chest as she poured another shot.

Sinnamon stood at the counter and drank shot after shot in an attempt to numb her pain. Before she realized it the bottle was halfway gone and she was drunk. To her surprise the liquor did nothing but make her feel worse. Again she broke down and cried. She collapsed on the floor and sulked in her misery and guilt. She thought about Shaquan and all he could be going through; She thought about Essence and again saw visions of her body laid out on the couch; She thought about Ms. Jones. Finally she thought about all the murders she committed.

Her thoughts led her back to the liquor cabinet. She stared at the kilo of cocaine then pulled it out and sat it on the counter. She stared at it and wondered if it was the answer to her problems; was it the escape she desperately needed. She grabbed a saucer and a steak knife from the dish rack then placed the saucer next to the coke; the knife she held in a shaky hand. Her mind screamed, "no" to the decision she was already committed to.

There was no turning back.

She pierced the rubber wrap with the tip of the knife then slit a small opening that spilt white powder onto the counter top. She sat the knife down, picked up the kilo and dumped a small hill of cocaine onto the saucer.

WASIIM

"This ought to do the trick," she slurred, then she buried her nose in the cocaine and snorted.

chapter
Five

"About time I got through to you," Gage said into his cell phone as he sat at the foot of his king size bed. He could see Arrissa leaned up against the headboard staring at him through the wide mirror that hung on the wall in front of him.

"Man it's so much going on right now," Esco said, "I had to turn my phone off so I could think. What's up though?"

"We need to talk," Gage said. "Where you at?"

"On my way to Libby's, then back up the way."

"Alright I'm about to throw something on then I'll meet you up the way. I'm all the way out my spot so it's gonna take me like a half an hour or so."

"I'll be at the barbershop. You want me to grab you something to eat?"

"Nah, I'm straight, just come out front when I blow the horn."

"Alright."

Gage disconnected the call then turned to Arrissa. "I'm about to go holler at Esco for a minute."

Arrissa folded her arms across her chest and gave Gage a stern look. "For what?"

Gage could sense an argument brewing. "Listen babe, I'm just trying to see what's going on alright?"

Arrissa let out a deep sigh then looked into Gage's eyes. "Please don't do anything stupid. It feels so good to have you here with me. I'd hate to lose you again."

"You're not going to lose me again, baby," Gage said, hoping he wasn't lying.

"What's up with you and Flip?" Gage asked the moment Esco

sat in the passenger seat of his car and slammed the car door shut. Gage drove the short distance to the corner and parked.

"You talked to him?" Esco asked.

"Yeah, and that nigga bugging. He talking about you and Mills had something to do with him getting robbed and shot. What's going on?"

"It's a small fucking world Gage," Esco said, shaking his head. "Believe it or not, my girl and her friend did that shit. Me and Mills ain't have nothing to do with it though. Out of all the niggas down Atlanta they run into that nigga."

Gage looked at Esco long and hard. "So you ain't have nothing to do with it?"

Esco scowled. "Come on dawg, you know me better than that. I ain't never been a grimy dude. I know shit look crazy but I swear to God I ain't have nothing to do with that shit. Don't let that nigga Flip poison ya mind."

Gage leaned back in his seat and relaxed. "My bad, dawg. I wasn't trying to assume the worst, but this situation is crazy." He paused then looked over at Esco. "That nigga killed Mills last night."

"How you know?"

"I was on the phone with the nigga when he did it. Esco this nigga was tripping. He threatened me and my wife. Boy was talking to me like I'm some type sucka. I feel like he forcing my hand."

"I feel you but you gotta fall back. You just came home. Don't worry about Flip. I'ma handle that nigga, you best believe that."

"So what's ya plan?"

"I ain't trying to get you involved so we ain't gonna speak on that."

"That nigga killed Mills and threatened my wife, I'm already involved."

"You sure?"

"What's the plan?"

"If you're serious about riding be ready tonight. I'ma call you when it's time. Just meet me up here."

"Alright, I'ma be waiting for ya call."

As Dirty As It Gets

Esco put his hand on the door handle prepared to make his exit. He looked over at Gage. "If you don't come through that's cool, Gage, I understand ya situation. Being a real nigga that gotta a lot of love for you, I advise you to sit this one out. Enjoy ya freedom and new life. You got too much to lose right now."

Gage took Esco's words in and contemplated taking his advice. He didn't want to lose his freedom again, but the strong current of revenge was taking him under. It had him convinced its sweetness was worth the risk.

I appreciate your concern, but my mind's already made up. Call me when you're ready."

Gage pulled up in front of the barbershop at a quarter to ten. Akon's voice blared through the car's speakers. The singer sung about how he would still kill if he were forced to. Gage could relate to every word Akon sung. Along with the music, his wife's pleas for him to stay home echoed in his mind, but her words weren't enough to calm the reawakened killer. He stepped out of the car into the chilly night dressed in black sweat pants, a black hoody, and a mind state for murder.

"What's good?" Gage said as he approached Esco, Beefy and Clark. The three of them were in front of the barbershop waiting on him. They too were dressed in black sweat pants and hoodies.

After Gage greeted everyone with the standard hood hand-shake and embrace, Esco asked, "You ready?"

"Always," Gage said.

"Alright, come on. The guns already in the car." Esco headed in the direction of a smoke gray '91 Chevy Lumina that sat alone on the corner.

At the car Esco got in behind the wheel, Clark took the front passenger seat while Gage and Beefy got in the back. Once seated, Gage noticed an army green duffle bag in the center of the seat between him and Beefy. Assuming that the bag held the guns, he unzipped it; his assumption was correct; the bag was loaded with four pieces of heavy steel. Gage pulled out an all-black AK 47. It was the first time he had such a destructive weapon in his possession and he decided it would be the gun he'd use.

"Damn," Beefy said when he saw the AK in Gage's hands.

"What else he got in there?" Beefy dug into the bag and pulled out the rest of the guns: a Mac-11, a Ruger Mini 14 and a 12 gauge shotgun. "Damn, Es, you ain't playing no games is you?"

"I told y'all I got enough guns to go over to Iraq," Esco said. "My white boy got military plugs. I ain't playing with that nigga Flip."

"I dig the fuck outta that," Clark said, then turned around in his seat. "Hand me one of those joints," he told Beefy.

Beefy gave Clark the Mac and kept the Mini 14 for himself. Gage continued to examine the AK. Over the years he'd heard many stories about the damage the gun caused. He knew it was a weapon designed to kill. Looking at it brought to surface the reality of what he was setting out to do. For a brief second he regretted his decision but again the current of revenge pulled him in and submerged him under its control.

Forty minutes passed before the Lumina made the turn onto Flip's street. Esco was about to circle the block until Gage's voice boomed throughout the silent car.

"There go Flip right there." Gage watched Flip walk out of his house then jog to the dark blue Dodge Caravan and get in behind the wheel.

Esco pulled into an empty parking space several cars behind the van Flip had climbed into. He put the Lumina in park, then turned the headlights out.

"Why you park?" Clark asked, frustration lacing his tone. "Pull up on the side of that nigga so I can knock his head off."

"Nah, we can't do it like that," Esco said. "We don't even know where Shaquan's at. He might be in the van, let's sit here for a minute and see what he does."

The Caravan's taillights came on, and then the van pulled out from its parking space, rode to the end of the block, and made a left turn.

"I wonder where he's going," Gage said to no one in particular.

"I don't know," Clark said, gripping the Mac tightly in his hand, "but I say we run up in that crib and see if the little boy's in there so we can do what we do."

"Let's wait a few minutes," Esco said. "I wanna see if he comes back."

Clark sighed. Patience wasn't his best quality. Gage on the other hand felt Esco's suggestion was a good one. If Flip were to come back to the house while they were inside there would be no way to avoid a gun battle; one he was sure Esco didn't want to engage in until after he had Shaquan back.

"I'm with Esco," Gage said. "We should wait a few minutes."

"They right," Beefy said.

Outnumbered, Clark sat back in his seat and said nothing. Gage could tell he was pissed.

Twenty minutes later there was still no sign of Flip or the van. Gage checked his watch. It was almost eleven o'clock. He looked out of the car's window. Surprisingly, the street was empty. Last time he remembered being at Flip's, the street was full of people.

"Let's go in there while the street's clear," Gage said. "I don't think Flip's coming back."

"That's what I'm talking about." Clark loaded a bullet into the Mac's chamber, preparing it to be fired.

Gage followed Clark's lead and cocked the AK back. He watched as a long pointed bullet appeared then disappeared into the chamber. His adrenaline pumped as he anticipated the next move.

"Pass me one of those guns," Esco said.

Gage passed him the shotgun.

Esco cocked it back then turned around and faced Gage and Beefy. "When we get in there I need y'all to search the spot. Gage, I want you to go upstairs, Beefy, you check the basement. Me and Clark gonna hold the first floor down alright?"

Everyone agreed without hesitation.

Clark was the first one out of the car. He held the Mac low by his side as he crept up to the house. Esco, Beefy and Gage trailed closely behind him. Once at the door Clark rang the doorbell then knocked.

"Who is it," a deep voice called out seconds later.

"Somebody order delivery." Clark said.

"Ain't nobody order no fucking food," the deep voice said, and then the door swung open and revealed a small man no older than eighteen.

"Well you shouldn't have opened the fucking door then," Clark said. He grabbed the smaller man by the collar of his shirt and shoved the barrel of the Mac in his face. He forced the young man back into the house. Gage and the others stormed in behind them with their guns pointed. Two more young men were sitting on the couch in front of a large screen TV playing PlayStation 3.

"Get the fuck on the floor," Esco yelled.

One look at the shotgun's barrel and both of the young men dropped their game controllers and laid face down on the floor.

"You too, pussy," Clark, said shoving the man that answered the door towards the two young men already laying face down. The man stumbled forward, caught his balance, and then glared back at Clark.

"Don't get yourself murdered, youngin'," Clark said. The young boy kept a hard look on his face as he laid down next to his comrades.

Beefy and Gage shot pass everyone to execute their parts of the plan. Gage ran up the steps two at a time. Once upstairs he searched from room to room. He was caught by surprise when he entered one of the rooms and spotted his onetime fling, Princess, trying to escape out of a window. She'd managed to get one leg out of the half opened window but was having a rough time squeezing the rest of her body out. When she spotted Gage and the large gun he held, her eyes doubled to twice their normal size.

Princess put her hands in the air as she straddled the windowsill. "Gage, please don't shoot me. I don't know what's going on. Flip just called me and asked me to watch the little boy." She pointed to the bed, which was adjacent to Gage.

Gage looked towards the direction Princess pointed and spotted a little boy he assumed was Shaquan laying duct taped on the bed. The little boy's eyes were shut tightly. It was obvious he was afraid. Gage turned his attention back to Princess. The thought of allowing her to escape crossed his mind but was erased when he heard a shotgun blast come from downstairs. He now thought about his freedom.

Esco heard the rapid fire of the AK and ran towards the steps.

As Dirty As It Gets

Before he could make his way up the staircase, he spotted Gage at the top of the stairwell carrying Shaquan in one hand, the AK in the other. As Gage descended the stairs Esco could see that Shaquan was duct taped and shaken. A new anger exploded in this chest. He looked from Shaquan to Gage. "Take him out to the car. We'll be done here in a second."

After watching Gage exit the front door, Esco walked over to where the young men lay. He stood over them with the shotgun gripped in his hands, it's stock pressed securely against his shoulder and the barrel aimed at the men.

"Y'all seen what I did to y'all friend," Esco said calmly. He pointed to the bloody mess that lay dead beside the young men. "Now I'ma ask again, where the fuck is Flip?"

"D-D-D—Delaware," one of the young men stammered.

Just as Esco received his answer Beefy walked into the living room. "I don't know what the fuck happened in the basement but its blood all over down there."

"Fuck it," Clark said. "We got what we came for." He pointed the Mac down at the young men then squeezed the trigger. Streams of bullets ripped through the men's bodies. When the gunfire stopped one of the men moaned out in pain.

Esco walked over to the crying man, pressed the shotgun barrel to the man's head, then pulled the trigger. Blood sprayed all over Esco's boots and sweat pants. He looked down at the three bullet ridden bodies satisfied. "Come on, we out."

"When I slow down toss that nigga out," Flip told Newz and Bone who were in the back of the van with Mills' body. They had just made the turn onto 23rd Street, where Off The Ave Barbershop was located. Bone slid the side door of the van open then he and Newz each took hold of a side of Mill's body. They held the body in an upright position, lifting it by the legs and under the arms.

Flip slowed the van down to almost a complete stop. He smiled when he saw the small crowd in front of the barbershop disperse. Everyone casually walked in separate directions.

"Dumb ass niggas think we the police," Flip said. "Hurry up and toss that nigga out."

Bone counted to three then he and Newz tossed Mills out of the van. The body landed on the windshield of a white Cadillac parked in front of the barbershop, rolled down onto the hood, leaving a crimson streak in the front of the car and then fell head first onto the concrete.

"Tell that nigga Esco he next," Flip yelled out of the driver's side window. He stepped on the gas, the tires screeched as the van took off. By the time Flip made it to the corner gunfire erupted. Bullets thumped against the back of the van then the back window shattered. Flip made a sharp turn onto Washington Street, barely missing a Ford Explorer. The van fishtailed but Flip quickly regained control.

When Flip reached the I-95 North exit, his cell phone rang. He snatched it from the center console. It was Esco.

"You decided to give that bitch up?" Flip said when he answered the phone.

"Nah, nigga, I just wanted to let you know I got my youngin' back."

"What?"

"You heard what the fuck I said. By the way, I'm up a body now."

Esco hung up.

Flip snapped his phone shut. "Damn, that nigga got the little boy from the spot. He probably killed Juice and them too. That nigga gonna pay for that shit though. I got something for his ass."

chapter six

When Gage pulled into his driveway the clock on his dashboard read 2:57 a.m. He put the car in park then turned the headlights and engine off. Gazing through the windshield, he could see that all the lights in his house were turned out. That surprised him. He ex-pected his wife to be up waiting for him to walk through the door. She had called five times since his return from Philly. Each time he sent her call to voicemail. Eventually he turned his cell phone off; there was too much going on for him to get into a shouting match with her.

He reclined the driver's seat back and tried to relax. When he closed his eyes he saw Princess. Her eyes absorbed him. She held her hands over top of her head in surrender as she straddled the windowsill. He had wanted to let her escape but couldn't. She was a witness.

He squeezed the trigger.

The assault rifle roared to life, jerking in his hands, as it spit shell casings from its release chamber onto the carpeted floor. Princess cried out in agony when the stream of bullets ripped into her chest. The window shattered. Shards of glass rained down on her, cutting gashes in her face as she fell out the window.

Gage released the trigger and walked over to what was left of the window's frame and looked out of it. Princess's broken body lay sprawled on the pavement two stories below. He backed away from the window then rushed over to the bed and grabbed Shaquan. He tossed the duct taped little boy

35

over his shoulder and made a beeline through the open bedroom door. When he reached the staircase, he saw Esco at the bottom step with the shotgun in hand.

As he descended the stairs he could see relief in Esco's eyes. Looking past Esco, Gage noticed the young men were still lay- ing face down on the floor. One had a hole in the back of his head big enough to pass a softball through. Blood pooled around his head, edging its way to the face of his friend that lay next to him. After Esco told him to take Shaquan to the car, Gage knew the rest of the young men would soon suffer the same fate.

In the car Gage carefully peeled the thick tape from Shaquan's mouth, then his wrists and ankles. After freeing him from his restraints, Gage noticed the little boy staring at him. He wondered what the child was thinking. The fear that was once painted on his small face was replaced by curiosity.

"She was nice to me," Shaquan said in a low voice. "How come you shot her?"

The innocence in Shaquan's voice reminded him of his own son, and he wondered if his actions would cause any psychological damage to the child. Remorse poked holes in his gangster persona. The new Gage re-emerged, sending the old him back into hiding. He now sat guilt ridden, wondering how, if ever, he could explain what happened inside that house to the wide-eyed little boy before him. Whatever the case, he knew no excuse would be sufficient for his Lord.

What sounded like a display of fireworks invaded the silence. Seconds later, it sounded as if a small bomb went off. Gage knew that was the shotgun. He looked from Shaquan to Flip's house. Esco, Clark and Beefy bolted out the front door. They rushed to the car and got in, each taking the same seat they sat in on their way to Philly.

Outside of the call Esco made to Flip, the ride back to Wilmington was silent. Gage sat in the backseat with the side of his head resting on the back door's window. He quietly supplicated to Allah for forgiveness.

"What the fuck happened out here?" Esco said.

As Dirty As It Gets

The sound of Esco's voice brought Gage out of his trance. He looked up to see that they were parked on 23rd and Jefferson St.

The familiar flashing of red and blue lights shifted his attention in the direction of the barbershop. Coroners, police, paramedics; everything about the scene spelled murder. He instinctively got out of the car and headed towards the red and blue lights. His stomach was in knots. Something told him that all the commotion had something to do with Flip.

"Yo, Gage," Esco called out.

Gage turned around to see Esco with his head sticking out of the driver's side window. "Call me soon as you find out what happened," Esco said. "I'm not staying around here with all this shit in the car."

Gage nodded to let Esco know that he heard his request, then watched as the Lumina pulled off. After the car made the left turn at the next corner, Gage made his way to the scene.

He soon found out what all the commotion was about. Just past the yellow tape that bordered the scene, he could clearly see his closest friend lying on the cold pavement outlined by white chalk. The police hadn't even bothered to cover Mills' body with a sheet.

Loud tapping jerked Gage out of his sleep. He looked to his left and through the driver's side window. His wife glared at him. Her head was covered with a long dark blue scarf. She stood up straight when their eyes locked and crossed her arms over her chest. Her over garment, the same color as her scarf, flared in the wind.

It was time to face the music.

Reluctantly, he popped open the car door and climbed out. He fixed his lips to apologize, but the words never escaped his throat. Arrissa walked off leaving him standing in the driveway. He looked to the sky; it was beginning to turn purple, an indication he needed to lead his family in the morning salaat (prayer).

When he walked into his house he was greeted by the smell of heated syrup and turkey bacon; another surprise. Maybe he wasn't in the doghouse after all. He jogged up the steps and headed to his bathroom. He brushed his teeth, performed Wudu, (purifying one- self with water in preparation of prayer) then went to his bedroom where he changed into a hunter green throbe. He gathered his discarded clothes, sneakers included, and took them downstairs with him in search of a trash bag. His search led him to the kitchen. Arrissa turned away from the stove when he walked in. Again their eyes locked. A blink later, hers rested on the bundle of clothes that was in his arms. He looked down at the ball of black fabric, embarrassed.

"As Salaamu alaykum," Gage said.

"Wa alaykum as Salaam," Arrissa replied dryly, then turned around to finish cooking.

Without another word Gage walked over to the sink, dropped the clothes at his feet, then crouched down and opened the cabinet. He found a roll of trash bags and ripped one free. He fanned it open then stuffed the clothes inside it.

"Leave it by the front door," Arrissa told him. "I'm going to Chester later on to get some new garbs, I'll throw it away up there."

"Thank you," Gage mumbled, tying the bag shut. Again he was embarrassed. Arrissa's offer let him know that she knew he did something foul.

"Go get Hakim so we can offer salaat," Arrissa said. "I'll be done in a minute. I'll meet y'all in the den."

Gage did as he was told. He and Hakim were going over the Al- Fatihah (the first chapter of the Quran), when Arrissa walked into the den. The family lined up then prayed. After the prayer they sat at the dining room table and ate breakfast. Once the food was done, Hakim was excused to his room.

Gage and Arrissa sat alone on opposite sides of the table.

"Have you told Sharron yet?" Arrissa asked.

Gage wondered how she knew.

As if reading his mind she said, "Wilmington's too small to keep secrets. That's why I was calling all night. I wasn't sure if you knew." She paused, then reached across the table and grabbed Gage by his hands. "How long is this going to last?"

"What?"

"Don't play stupid, Mujahid," Arrissa said, addressing Gage by his Muslim name.

Gage sighed. "I don't know."

Arrissa snatched her hands away then sunk back into her seat. "So I have to lose my husband too?"

"Ain't nobody say that."

"Some things don't have to be said to be clear." Gage massaged his temples. "Baby, not right now."

"Then when?"

Gage banged his fist on the table. The dishes rattled from the impact. "I said not right now, Arrissa. Damn, just leave me alone for a minute. I just saw my best friend laid out in the middle of the street, and gotta find a way to tell his wife she ain't never gonna see him again."

"I understand that, but I'm worried about my husband right now. You've barley been home two weeks and you're already back to your old ways. So yes I'm concerned. I don't want to lose you again, Mujahid. I love you."

Gage huffed, then in a gentler tone said, "Let me take a shower then call Sharron...we'll talk after that." Before Arrissa could reply, he was on his feet and leaving the table.

Upstairs Gage showered and then dressed in a pair of basketball shorts and a tee shirt. He sat at the foot of his bed with his cell phone in his hand. Sharron's name and number were on the small screen, but he had yet to push the send button to put the call through. He could only imagine how Sharron was going to respond to the news. Finally after several minutes of hesitation he pushed the button and called.

"Hello," Sharron answered on the first ring.

"What's up, Sharron, this is Gage."

"Oh my God, Gage, I'm so happy to hear from you. I haven't heard from Mills in three days. Have you?"

Gage took a deep breath. "That's why I'm calling."

chapter seven

Sinnamon stood at the sink in her bathroom with a towel wrapped around her wet body. She leaned closer to the mirror that hung over top of the sink and studied her face. Dark circles were beneath her blood shot eyes. She spent her nights tossing and turning, trying to escape the images of death. A task only accomplished when her mind was chemically altered and the world she lived in no longer existed.

Unhappy with her reflection, Sinnamon sighed and turned away from the mirror. Her eyes landed on her purse, which sat next to the toilet. The thought of what lay in the hidden compartment she managed to make one sleepless night, drew her to it. She pulled the toilet lid down, sat on it, and then placed the purse on her lap. She glanced over at the bathroom door and saw that it was locked. She then dumped contents of the purse at her feet, dug her fingers into the small slit in the bottom of the purse's lining and pulled out one of the several small baggies of cocaine she put together. A wave of guilt crashed down on her but was quickly dragged away by a current of rationalization, her justification to get high. Today she would have to endure the ramifications of death and couldn't imagine doing it with a sober mind.

She sat the purse next to the junk she dumped out of it and sifted through the small pile. It didn't take long for her to find what she was looking for. She unwrinkled a twenty-dollar bill, rolled it into a neat straw then flipped open a compact mirror. A razor fell into her lap. She sat the mirror next to it, ripped the baggie open with her teeth and dumped the potent powder onto the glass surface. Using the razor, she separated the cocaine into two lines then

As Dirty As It Gets

put Andrew Jackson to one of her nostrils. She vacuumed up one of the lines then quickly switched Jackson to her other nostril and repeated the process. Afterwards she threw her head back, closed her eyes and rode the train of temporary pleasure.

Once the initial rush of her high settled, she cleaned up the evidence of her indiscretions, then took her place back at the sink and stared into the mirror. She saw traces of white powder at the edges of her nostrils and quickly wiped her face with a damp cloth. Once more, she peered into the mirror; and this time, all traces of her secret were gone.

"You okay?" Esco asked Sinnamon the moment she stepped into their bedroom. He was across the room, standing in front of their full-length mirror, dressed in the same color she would be wearing. Black.

"I'm fine," she said. To avoid Esco's gaze, she cast her eyes to the carpeted floor and headed for her walk-in closet.

From behind her, Esco said, "I'ma run Shaquan by my mom's then I'll be back."

When she heard the bedroom door shut, she sighed in relief. Now she had more time to pull herself together. She removed a Donna Karen skirt, blouse and blazer from a couple of hangers then strolled out of the closet to begin her ritual of getting dressed. After she put on her clothes she sat on the small stool in front of her vanity table and started in on her makeup. Once her makeup was applied, and her hair combed till it fell like black silk down her back, she looked at herself in the vanity mirror and smiled. The reflection staring back at her took her back to the day Essence taught her how beautiful she was. Tears attempted to build in her eyes, but she suppressed them and shook the memory. Unconsciously she rubbed her nose and sniffled.

"You gonna make ya nose red you keep rubbing it like that."

Sinnamon jumped at the sound of Esco's voice. Lost in her thoughts she hadn't heard him enter the room. Before she could reply, she felt his arms around her body. His reflection now shared the mirror with hers. They made a beautiful couple.

"When are we going to get married?" she asked his reflection.

"I don't know, I guess when this beef dies down."

"I've been doing a lot of thinking and I don't want to wait too long. Life's too short, baby. Look at Essence; we're about to go to her funeral." Tears pearled in the corners of her eyes then fell one by one. She turned and faced Esco. "I'm sorry, baby."

"For what?"

"Everything. This whole situation is my fault."

"It's alright, baby. I got you. When it's all said and done, we gonna come out on top. You hear me?" Esco's confidence made her believe him, and for the moment she was comforted by something other than her habit.

The limo parked in front of Congo's on Twenty-fourth and Market Street. Sinnamon shuddered when she saw the funeral home through the limo's tinted window. The stone structure had the appearance of a small medieval castle and had the nerve to be next to a playground. She wondered who would put a place for the dead next to a place where children played. Her aggravation grew at the sight of all the people filing into the building. Each of them wearing their best, some smiling, others appearing sincerely sad; an emotion none of them could possibly really feel. They were all strangers. She was Essence's only friend.

"You sure you're going to be able to handle this?" Esco asked from his seat next to Sinnamon.

She cut her eyes at him. Venom flooded her mouth but was quickly swallowed before her tongue was able to spew it.

"I really have no choice," she said. "But after we view her, I want to sit in the back."

The chauffer opened the door. Sinnamon was the first to step out. Her body shivered the moment she planted her stilettos on the pavement. She wasn't sure if it was from the chill in the air or her nervousness. A woman going into Congo's waved in her direction. She didn't return the gesture. Instead, she rolled her eyes, nestled closely to Esco's side, and then let him lead her to the entrance of the building. A man wearing a black suit held the building's door open. He greeted the line of people with a nod and offered them obituaries. Sinnamon declined the one offered to her. Essence's sister, the same woman who denied Sinnamon any input on it, had prepared the thin program. She told Sinnamon that putting together

As Dirty As It Gets

an obituary was a job for family members only, not associates. Sinnamon was a hair away from spitting on the ungrateful bitch. Essence would've been buried naked and in a cardboard box if Sinnamon hadn't paid for the funeral and everything that came with it.

The atmosphere inside of the funeral home was just as cold as the outside. Sinnamon's trembling intensified as the line for the viewing moved forward. The closer she came to front of the funeral home, the harder it was to walk. A break in-between the people in front of her revealed a glimpse of a pearl white casket. Her body temperature shot up and she became light headed. Grief pooled in her eyes then streamed down her face in the form of salty tears. She wanted to turn around and leave, but she pushed forward anyway. She had to say good-bye.

When she reached the casket, she felt as if a python had wrapped around her body and squeezed. Essence's honey-brown complexion was two shades darker and dull. Sinnamon caressed her face. The feel of Essence's cold skin was a chilly reminder of death. Esco's presence wasn't enough to comfort her. She felt weak. The words she wanted to say came out jumbled. She cried. She screamed. Her knees buckled. Esco held her up and tried to usher her away but she resisted, yelling words that sounded foreign.

She stood at Essence's casket for a full minute before she pulled herself together enough to speak. She took a deep breath. "I'm sooo sorry," she said. "I should've been there. I know I should've been there. I could've done something." Her words came out choppy and cracked. "I'ma miss you so much. Sisters even after death. I love you." She leaned over and kissed Essence on the cheek. Her tears rained down into the casket, leaving a trace of her soul with the only sister she knew. She walked away from the casket with an irreplaceable piece of her heart ripped from her chest. She sat quietly in her seat at the back of the room, yearning for a dose of escapism. She couldn't wait to go home and lock herself back in the bathroom.

When the service ended, Sinnamon and Esco followed the trail of people exiting the building. Outside, the bright sun did nothing

43

to change her dark mood. She felt as cold as the winter wind that swirled dead leaves around the front of the building.

"Get down, get down, he has a gun!" A man suddenly yelled.

Sinnamon's eyes locked in on a man who was hanging out of the sliding door of a dark blue Dodge Caravan. The image seemed unreal. He gripped the largest gun she'd ever seen in her life. Everything seemed to slow down, and she froze in fear when the van stopped in front of the funeral home.

A burst of gunfire ripped through the air. Bullets mowed down the innocent and ricocheted off the stone building. Esco pushed Sinnamon to the ground then threw himself on top of her. The screams of the crowd and gunshots rang loudly in Sinnamon's ears. She closed her eyes, wishing she were somewhere else. She'd never been shot at before and she didn't know what to do. Just as fast as the gunshots started, they stopped. The tires of the van screeched and then there was silence.

Sinnamon opened her eyes. The consequences of her past were all around her, and she wondered what she had gotten herself into.

chapter eight

"Those niggas is starting to get on my fucking nerves," Esco told Beefy and Gage, from his seat in one of the barber chairs in OFF THE AVE.

"I feel you," Gage said. "I had to tell Mills' wife about him yesterday. What we gonna do about these niggas?"

"I don't know," Esco said, "but we need to come up with some-thing soon. Them niggas is reckless."

"Where that nigga bitch at?" Beefy asked. "Something happens to her, he'll put himself on frontline and stop sending his flunkies."

"We can't do nothing to her," Gage said. "She ain't got nothing to do with this shit."

"What, you forgot he trying to kill my girl?" Esco asked.

"I feel you, but that don't make it right," Gage said. "Besides, I ain't trying to be responsible for any more unnecessary deaths."

"What you suggest then?" Beefy said, laying back in his seat. "Cuz we gonna end up with a million years shooting out with them niggas every time they choose to come through."

Gage thought for a moment then a smile crept across his face. "Night on Broad. That's his favorite spot. Ain't no way he in Philly and not going there."

"Now you onto something," Esco said. "I think Lil Kenny know a couple bitches that work there. I'ma get with him and see if we can set something up."

"How the fuck y'all miss?" Flip said, pacing in front of Bone and Newz who were seated on the hotel room's bed.

WASIIM

Ever since the night his house in Philly was invaded, Flip had been hiding out in a Days Inn just outside the city.

"Nigga, you act like we ain't try," Newz said.

Bone chuckled. "We hit a couple people though."

"That's the fucking problem. You little mutha-fuckas think everything's a fucking joke. I need to send you mutha-fuckas to the gun range." Flip plopped down onto an under-stuffed armchair and glared at Bones and Newz. He couldn't believe they messed up such an easy hit.

"I don't know why you looking at us like that," Bone said. "You should've came up with a better plan. That drive by shit been played. We need to just walk up on one of them niggas and give 'em a couple head shots."

"I hear that, gangsta," Flip said. "But it ain't gonna be that easy, especially now. Them mutha-fuckas gonna be on point."

"So what's next?" Newz asked.

"Nothing for y'all right now," Flip said. "Just fall back for a minute. I'ma put my niggas from Night on Broad on them pussies."

"Who, Pee-Wee and Noble?" Bone asked.

"Yeah," Flip said. "I'ma hit them niggas below the belt. It wouldn't be right if I didn't respond properly to what they did at my spot." He pulled his cell phone from his pocket and checked the time. "They should be at the club now. Let's slide through there so I can holla at them."

Flip got up from the chair, snatched his keys from the small table next to it and headed to the door. Bone and Newz got up and followed behind him. Outside in the hotel's parking lot, they walked to a dark-green Yukon Denali. It's candy paint and 24-inch chrome rims shined beneath the streetlights. Flip deactivated the trucks alarm system then tossed the keys to Bone. "Don't crash my shit."

The music in the club vibrated the walls. Flip noticed two top-less women sitting on stools at the bar staring in his direction when he walked into the club. The women moved their bodies suggestively to the beat of the song, but he walked by them without a second glance. The bitter taste of

As Dirty As It Gets

Sinnamon and Essence was still on his tongue. He would have to do a little investigating before he even thought about entertaining them. Bone and Newz on the other hand joined the women at the bar.

When Flip walked into the lap dance area, he scanned the room for Pee-Wee and Noble. His eyes were greeted by colorful thongs, ass, titties and longhaired weaves. Women he knew. He grabbed a slim, brown-skinned stripper by her waist and pulled her to him. She giggled and grinded her ass against his groin.

"Butter, you seen Pee-Wee or Noble?" He asked.

Butter pointed across the room, "Pee-Wee over there."

Flip looked in the direction Butter pointed and saw Pee-Wee sit-ting on a couch with a stripper on his lap.

"Who that bitch, she new?"

"Yeah," Butter replied then held out her hand. "Gimme some money."

Flip pulled a thick knot of cash from his pocket and peeled off a crisp hundred-dollar bill. "We fucking tonight. Ya number still the same?"

"Yeah, and make sure you call me. Don't be bullshitting, Flip."

"I got you." He smacked Butter on her ass then walked over to

Pee-Wee and sat next to him. "What's up?"

"Pussy and ass," Pee Wee said. "Ain't nothing new."

The music faded but quickly bounced back with a new song. The stripper got up from Pee-Wee's lap and snatched the twenty dollar bill he dangled in her face. She tucked it in her metallic gray G-string and walked off.

"Bitch, you better bring that yellow ass back over here," Pee-Wee shouted over the music. "A lap dance ain't but ten dollars. I know you see my peoples sitting over here. Get ya sexy ass to work."

The stripper sucked her teeth. "My name ain't bitch, it's Cream, mutha-fucka."

Flip pulled out his knot again and peeled off another crisp

47

hundred. He held the big face president between his index and middle fingers. Cream tried to snatch it but he yanked it back. "Only if we can call you bitch."

"Ya know what, fuck both you petty mutha-fuckas." Cream stormed off.

Flip watched as her ass jiggled with each step she took. When she was out of sight, he burst out laughing. "That bitch was mad as shit. You see how red her face got?"

Pee-Wee laughed with him. "I see you ain't lose ya touch being down in the country all that time."

"Never that, but listen, I got some work for you and Noble. Where he at?"

"At his spot with his baby mom."

"He in for the night?"

"Yeah, he said she bugging. What's the look though? I'll run shit by him tomorrow."

"Remember them niggas from Delaware I was fucking with?"

Pee-Wee scowled. "I ain't killing no Muslims, Flip. You on your own with that shit."

Flip sucked his teeth. "Man go head with that bullshit, this war.

Remember when I got shot?"

Pee-Wee nodded.

"Come to find out," Flip said, "they the ones that put the line on me. Them niggas foul."

"I hear that, but I'm still Muslim despite all the bullshit I do, and killing another Muslim ain't something I can stomach."

"I dig that but listen, the mutha-fucka I want you to get at ain't even Muslim. This just a reply for what they did at my spot. They killed three of my young boys and this babe I was cool with. She was like a little sister to me."

"I heard about that shit," Pee-Wee said, staring intently at Flip.

"I'ma ride with you, but no Muslims Flip."

"Listen, I already know. No Muslims."

As Dirty As It Gets

"So what's the plan?"

Flip smiled like the devil himself. "Murder."

chapter

nine

Gage exhaled as he pushed the 225lbs of steel weights off his chest. The muscles in his arms and chest bulged from the pressure. He tightened his grip around the bar then inhaled as he slowly brought the weight back down to his sternum. Again he pushed the weight up with force, blowing out a steam of frustration from the pit of his stomach. He slammed the bar down on its resting place then sat upright on the bench. Sweat collected around his eyebrows and trailed from his temples to his thick beard. His breathing was heavy but controlled. His heart held the constant beat like the boots of a disciplined soldier marching off to war, but his mind was at ease. The small gym in his basement always served its purpose.

An annoying buzzing interrupted Gage's focus. He looked towards the direction the noise came from and saw his cell phone flashing on the seat of the leg machine across from him. He got up from the bench and grabbed the phone. Blood torpedoed through his veins when he saw that it was Flip.

"What the fuck you want?" Gage said.

"Chill, Gage. I come in peace."

"Peace!" Gage's voice echoed in the small room. "What the fuck you mean peace. I gotta bury Mills tomorrow."

"I know, but hear me out."

"For what, nigga? You already crossed the line, what the fuck is there to hear?" Gage paced from wall to wall.

"Listen, Gage, all I'm saying is this shit ain't got nothing to do with you. You was in jail when shit went down, so you don't even know what's going on. Ain't no point getting involved in some shit you don't know nothing about. Them niggas crossed me first."

As Dirty As It Gets

"That's neither here nor there, Flip. You called me popping fly and did that shit to Mills while I was on the phone. That was like my fucking brother."

"We was all like brothers," Flip shouted. "And you know the rules: you do dirt, you get dirt. Look at what you did to your *real* brother."

Gage stopped his stride. Flip's words hit him in his gut harder than a cannon ball. "Don't ever bring my fucking brother up," he said. "You hear me, nigga? I'll fucking kill you."

Flip chuckled. "Kill me, huh? Why, cause the truth hurts?"

"That shit was different."

"Different? Cause he was a rat? Them mutha-fuckas almost had me killed."

"You don't know that."

"How don't I know, Gage. You know damn well that shit don't look right. I seen Esco with them bitches with my own eyes, not nobody telling me the shit. I seen it for myself."

"What's that gotta do with Mills?"

"Everything. Esco ain't know where I stayed down south. So like I told you before, Mills had to tell him. Just keep it real with me. If you was in my shoes, what would you have done?"

Gage didn't respond.

"You can't even answer me. But listen, I ain't even gonna keep arguing over a dead issue. I'm just extending my hand again in peace. This shit ain't got nothing to do with you, Gage. You ain't got but one time to cross me. Stay the fuck out the way." Flip dis-connected the call.

Gage snapped his phone shut then flopped down onto the seat of the leg machine.

"You okay?" Gage heard Arrissa say behind him.

He turned around and saw his wife standing at the gym's door. She was dressed to workout. Terry cloth shorts revealed her thick but toned legs, and a sports bra showcased her flat stomach while accentuating her firm breasts. She walked over to him and sat on his lap. Her soft backside absorbed his concrete structure. Her smell, a pleasant scent of warm vanilla, reminded him of peace and eased his tension.

"I don't even know, babe." He said, wrapping his arms around Arrissa's waist.

"What's going on?" she asked.

"Too much." Gage sighed then told Arrissa a little about his conversation with Flip.

"I understand how you feel, baby," Arrissa said. "But Flip's right, the situation does seem suspect." She turned her head and looked Gage in the eyes. "Besides, baby, you made a promise to me, and your son, and most importantly you made a promise to Allah. You have to walk away from this nonsense."

"How can I just up and walk away from something like this? Mills was like my brother."

"You have to think about your family. What will me and Hakim do if you go back to jail or die behind this foolishness?" You getting involved isn't going to bring Mills back. All it's going to do is destroy all we worked so hard to get. You had 56 years to do...56 long years, Mujahid. But you're free now."

"Walking away is easier said than done, Arrissa. I don't know if I can do it."

"Mujahid, this isn't fair to me and your son. Please think about us. Let's just move. I don't want to lose you again." Arrissa's eyes watered then a single tear fell.

Gage placed his hand on her cheek then used his thumb to brush away the trail of water the tear left behind.

Arrissa grabbed Gage's hand, held it tightly and looked her deep in his eyes. "How many favors of your Lord will you deny?"

chapter Ten

Sinnamon sat on her knees with her head hung over top of the toilet. Chunks of food spewed from her mouth and splashed into the water. Her body relaxed then she heaved again. She stiffened as another flow of soggy food spewed from her mouth. Sweat pooled at the back of her neck and in between her breast. She gripped the rim of the toilet when she felt another wave coming. She expelled the rest of the contents in her stomach then pushed down on the toilet seat to help herself up from the floor. Her body felt weak. She braced herself against the sink and looked into the mirror. Her face was pale.

"What's wrong with me," she said out loud. This was the third time she threw up that day. "I know what I need." She pulled the toilet seat down then sat on it and placed the purse she kept in the bathroom on her lap. After pulling out two baggies of cocaine, she prepared four lines and snorted them. The sudden rush relieved her of the nausea. She sat on the toilet for a few minutes then noticed a drop of blood on her tee-shirt. She held her head back then ripped some tissues from the toilet paper holder and stuffed them in her nose. When the bleeding stopped she cleaned herself and the bathroom then went into her bedroom. Nausea bombarded her again and her head began to spin. She laid down hoping the feeling would go away.

It didn't.

"I'm losing my mind cooped up in this house," she shouted, kicking her legs and swing her arms wildly. Thoughts drummed in her head causing it to ache. So many mistakes. So many regrets. So many lives destroyed. It was all her fault. Nothing good seemed promised. Death was inevitable. She was afraid. She didn't want to die. She wanted life.

"Oh my God." She jumped off the bed and began to dress.

"Shaquan put some clothes on, we're going to the store," she yelled to Shaquan who was in his bedroom.

"Okay," Shaquan yelled back.

Sinnamon stuffed her feet into a pair of Nikes she never wore before. They felt awkward. This was her first time wearing sneakers in months. Once dressed, she brushed her hair back into a tight ponytail.

"Shaquan, you ready?" She asked, slipping on a waist length leather jacket. She hoisted a tan leather bag that matched the jacket over her shoulder then left the room. Shaquan was already waiting for her. They made their way down the steps then outside.

Sinnamon breathed in the fresh air. It was warmer than normal. The sun peaked from the clouds and became her spotlight. Her nausea was gone. She hopped into her Bentley and pulled off with a smile.

The ride to the store was short. It was only up the street from her house. She pulled into the store's small parking lot and parked. She stepped out the car and opened the back door for Shaquan. He bounced out and ran into the store. Sinnamon smiled and unconsciously placed a hand on her stomach.

"Get whatever you want," she told Shaquan when they entered the store. He dashed to the candy aisle causing Sinnamon to smile again. She stood behind the only person in line at the counter. When the man paid for his things he nodded at her and headed for the door.

The store clerk, an older white woman who wore a friendly smile on her face, turned her attention to Sinnamon and asked, "How can I help you?"

"Do you have any First Response Pregnancy tests?" As soon as the words left her mouth, Sinnamon noticed the clerk's gaze shift to her hands. The big rock on her left ring finger was hard to miss.

"That's so wonderful you're married," the clerk said then turned around to find the test.

Sinnamon spotted the test before the clerk. "It's at the bottom."

As Dirty As It Gets

The clerk reached down and grabbed the test then turned back to the counter. Shaquan came running up behind Sinnamon with an armful of candy. She moved out his way so he could put his load on the counter.

"Second time around?" The clerk asked with a giggle.

"No," Sinnamon said, "but hopefully it's the first."

The clerk scanned everything, placed the items in a plastic bag, and handed the bag to Sinnamon. "Thirty-eight fifty sweetie."

Sinnamon dug in her pocketbook and pulled out two twenties. She handed them to the clerk then waited for her change.

"Congratulations, sweetie," the clerk said, handing Sinnamon her change. She looked down at Shaquan. "And don't you eat all that candy in one sitting, handsome. You're gonna have a big ol' tummy ache."

"Have a nice day," Sinnamon said on her way out the door.

The moment Sinnamon walked through her front door she took the pregnancy test out of the plastic bag then handed the bag filled with candy over to Shaquan. He took off up the steps swinging the bag in his hand.

Sinnamon was right behind him. She darted into her bathroom and shut the door. She couldn't wait to take the test. Nervousness and excitement caused her to not only pee on the stick but her hand as well. When she was done she cleaned herself then flushed the toilet. She sat the test on the ledge of the bathtub then washed her hands.

Five minutes the instructions said. She chewed on her bottom lip as she waited. Anticipation was eating her alive. The world seemed to spin a lot slower. Every time she peeked her head out the bathroom door to look at the digital clock on her night stand the numbers were the same.

Finally, after what seemed like five days, five minutes passed. Sinnamon lifted the test from the tub and looked at the results.

Positive.

A new charge of energy flowed through her. She jumped up and down and danced. Life finally seemed to over shadow death. Hope was growing in her stomach. She couldn't wait to call Esco. She left out the bathroom to find her cell phone but stopped in her tracks. Her smile faded. Tears began to fall. She dropped to the floor and screamed. No words, just the sounds of a wounded lioness. She rubbed her stomach, trying to console who's inside it. What would she do if her drug use killed her baby?

Chapter Eleven

"I don't think I'm going to make it to the dinner." Sharron folded her arms across her chest then leaned back against the driver's side door of the Chrysler 300 she rented at the airport.

"I thought you said ya flight don't leave until later on tonight," Gage said as he stood in front of her.

Sharron glanced down the street in the direction of the Masjid. Her husband's body was in there, shrouded in white linen prepared to become one with the earth.

"The Janazah (Muslim Funeral Service) was enough for me." Her voice cracked. "I can't take any more." She wiped the fresh tears that pooled in her eyes with the back of a gloved hand.

"You gonna be okay?"

Sharron took a deep breath. "I'm trying. I think I need to take a ride so I can clear my mind."

"I understand." Gage placed his hand on her shoulder and looked into her eyes. "Don't worry, I'ma hunt them niggas down. I promise."

"That's not what I want. All the violence needs to stop and you need to stay as far away from the streets as possible. Set the bar for the young Muslims coming up behind you and change. You've been through so much. Share your story, raise your son, and be there for your wife. Don't let Mills' death suck you back into the madness."

"Everybody keeps telling me the same thing, but it's hard. I might just pack up and leave. I can't stay around all this."

"That'd be for the best," Sharron said. "Mills has a bunch of houses down Atlanta. You and your family will always have some where to stay."

"I'll let you know if I decide to take you up on that offer."

"Insha Allah (God willing)," Sharron said.

"Well I'ma let you get going, sis, we still have to go to the cemetery for the burial." Gage gave Sharon a hug. "Let me know if you need anything, and call me when you get to the airport so I can know you made it there alright."

"I will." Sharron deactivated the Chrysler's alarm system and the doors unlocked. Gage opened the driver's door for her and she got in. "You just hurry up and make that move with your family."

"Alright, Sharron I got you. As salaamu alaykum."

"Wa alaykum as salaam." Sharron pulled her door shut then watched Gage walk back towards the Masjid. Dozens of Muslim men were out in front of it. All of them reminded her of Mills in some way. She started the car then backed out of the parking spot and looked towards the Masjid for the last time.

"I love you."

Sharron drove with no destination. Every turn she made was without thought. It was as if the car drove itself. Before she knew it she found herself headed to a park she used to go to when she was a child. She looked at the dashboard to see how much time she had before her flight.

"Dammit!" she said when she spotted the check that she was supposed to give Mills' mother. It was taped to the dashboard as a reminder. She grabbed her cell phone from the passenger seat and dialed Mills' mother.

"I ain't feeling this shit, Flip," Pee-Wee said from the passenger seat of the black Dodge Magnum.

Flip gripped the steering wheel annoyed, but said nothing. He continued to follow the car in front of him. The car and its driver was his only concern. Pee-Wee's personal feelings meant nothing.

"You know niggas don't be running around killing bitches," Noble said from the backseat.

"Fuck that," Pee-Wee said. "I told this nigga at the club I ain't killing no Muslims."

"Listen," Flip said through gritted teeth. "I told you, the mutha-fucking bitch ain't Muslim."

"She's garbed up like one though, Flip," Pee-Wee said. "How the fuck you know she ain't Muslim?"

"Mutha-fucka, cause I said so."

"Who the fuck is you talking to like that." Pee-Wee gripped the butt of the black Desert Eagle that sat on his lap.

Flip pulled a Chrome .45 from under his thigh. "Don't grab ya gun like that, Pee-Wee."

"Why is you playing with my fucking intelligence, Flip." Ice layering Pee-Wee's words.

"Listen," Flip spoke in a calm tone. "Ain't nobody playing with ya fucking intelligence. If anything you niggas is playing with mine. Y'all said y'all was gonna ride with me. We *supposed* to be peoples and I'm paying y'all double at that."

"A million dollars wouldn't be enough," Pee-Wee said.

"You niggas need to chill the fuck out," Noble cut in.

Pee-Wee looked back at Noble. "Nah, this nigga need to chill, tryna kill Muslims."

"Damn, Pee-Wee, I said she ain't Muslim. She only dress like that 'cause she coming from the funeral. Stop acting like this new to you. Bitches do that shit all the time." Flip looked over at Pee-Wee. "What, you don't trust me?"

"Yeah, I trust you," Pee-Wee answered. "I trust you to be nut ass Flip."

Flip grinned.

"See, I ain't fucking with you," Pee-Wee said. "I can't do it."

"You know what?" Flip said. "Fuck it!" He stepped on the gas. "I don't even know why I hired you all of a sudden sentimental mutha-fuckas anyway. I'll do the shit myself."

Flip caught up to the Chrysler. He pulled up alongside it and turned his wheel hard to the right. The cars collided. The Chrysler swerved then smacked into the back of a parked pick-up truck. Flip slammed on his breaks. The Magnum's tires screamed as they skidded across the pavement then came to a stop.

"What the fuck is you doing?" Pee-Wee shouted. "It's broad daylight, you don't see all those people out there?"

"Fuck'em." Flip pulled the hood of his coat over his head,

opened the car door and jumped out clutching the .45 in his hand. He jogged over to the Chrysler. It's front end was stuck under the bed of a truck and smashed. He aimed the large gun at the driver's side window. Sharron, bleeding from her nose and mouth, fought with the Chrysler's airbag.

He squeezed the trigger. The window shattered.

He walked closer to the car.

Sharron tried to crawl her way to the passenger door. He squeezed the trigger again and again.

Sharron screamed.

He continued to squeeze. When the screaming stopped, he ran around to the passenger door and used the sleeve of his coat to open it. Sharron was sprawled across the middle console and passenger seat. Flip fired two rounds into the back of her skull then jogged back to the Magnum, got in and pulled off.

Chapter Twelve

Gage was about to get into his car when his cell phone rang. He looked at the caller ID, Mills' mother was calling. "Hello," he answered.

"Anthony! I was talking to Sharron then — then— I don't know.
Oh my God, I think something happened to her. It was so loud."

Gage's heart began to pound, "What was loud? What happened?"

"I don't know. It sounded like a crash, then gunshots. She was screaming. She was supposed to meet me —"

"Meet you where?" Gage got into his car and started the engine.

"At the park."

"What park."

"Hanes's. She said she was on her way to Hanes's Park, that she just crossed Washington Street Bridge. Anthony, she was screaming so loud. I know something bad happened to her, I just know it."

"Okay, this what I'ma do." Gage pulled out from his parking space. "I'm about to head in that direction to see if I see her. Maybe she got into an accident. I'll call you if I find out something."

"Okay, you make sure you're safe, Anthony."

"I'll call you in a few." Gage disconnected the call then sat the phone on his lap. He drove as fast as he could and only slowed down at stop signs. Sirens echoed from a distance. The closer he came to Washington Street, the louder the sirens became. Three police cruisers darted past him when he was forced to stop at a red light. He felt his heart thump twice for every second that passed.

WASIIM

The light turned green.

He turned onto Washington Street and pressed down on the gas pedal a little more. Two more police cruisers shot past him with their emergency lights flaring. He followed them past Wilmington hospital and over the Washington Street Bridge. Ambulance lights flickered a few blocks away. A lump formed in his throat. His heart thumped harder. A block away from where he saw the collection of flashing lights, a uniformed officer stood in the middle of the road detouring traffic. He pointed to Gage's left. Gage made the turn, found an empty parking space and parked. He jumped out of his car and jogged back around towards the scene.

"Hey you!" The officer that was directing traffic yelled. "You can't go down there."

Gage looked at him and sped up.

"Stop!"

Gage continued to run. He spotted the back of Sharron's rental and ran faster. There was a crowd of people gathered on the sidewalk. He forced himself through them but was stopped when he tried to duck under the yellow tape that blocked off the scene.

"Slow down buddy." A black man wearing a gray suit with no tie grabbed Gage by his arm.

Gage snatched away from him.

"That's my sister's car!" Gage said, looking the man up and down. A badge attached to a sliver chain hung from his neck.

"You sure that's your sister's car?" "Yeah—no—it's a rental. Her name's Sharron."

The man fished a small notepad from the top pocket of his blazer and flipped it open. "Sounds about right." He stuck out a slender hand. "My name's Detective Johnson, do you mind coming with me and answering a few questions?"

Gage looked at the Detective's hand, then around him to Sharron's rental. All its doors were open and he could see that the driver's door window was shattered.

A man in a tan colored suit took pictures of the car from different angles while another man, this one dressed in a black suit, placed yellow markers with black numbers on them on the ground. The highest number Gage saw was eight.

As Dirty As It Gets

"No," Gage said. "I don't want to answer no questions. I want to see what's up with Sharron."

"If you come with me, I'll tell you what you need to know. This isn't the place for that though."

"I ain't going to no police station."

"Fine, we can go over there to my car." Detective Johnson pointed across the street to a dark blue 2005 Crown Victoria.

Gage looked at the car then back at the detective.

"I ain't got no info for you."

Detective Johnson scowled. "I didn't say you did. But if you want to know what's going on with your sister, I suggest you follow me." He walked away from Gage and towards his car.

Gage stared at the detective's back for a moment then followed him. "We can talk outside, I ain't getting in your car."

"I understand." Detective Johnson sat on the car's hood. "First things first, what's your name?"

"Do all that matter? I just wanna know what's up with my sister."

Detective Johnson took a deep breath. "Someone murdered her."

Gage felt a hot tear trail down his face. He sat next to the detective and tried to collect himself.

"What happened?" Gage said.

"We're not really sure," Johnson said. "Whatever happened, happened not even fifteen minutes ago. How did you know to come here?"

Gage wiped his face with the sleeve of his throbe.

"Her mother-in-law called me. Said she was talking to her, then heard a crash and screaming." He paused. "This shit is crazy. We just left her husband's funeral."

"Marcus Miller's?"

Gage looked over at the detective. "How you know?"

Johnson wrote something in his notepad. "I'm working on his case too." He stopped writing and looked at Gage. "You think this has something to do with his murder?"

"I don't know what's going on." Gage got up from the hood of the car. The detective did the same.

"I think you're lying."

"I think you need to go do your job."

Johnson dug into the inside pocket of his blazer and pulled out a black and white business card. "I don't have time to go back and forth with you right now." He tucked the card in the front pocket of Gage's throbe. "Call me when you're ready to talk."

Gage took the card from his pocket and tossed it on the ground. He turned his back on the detective and walked away. As he walked back to his car he took out his cell phone and called Esco.

"What's good?" Esco answered.

"Meet me up the way, somebody killed Sharron."

"I'm on my way."

Gage parked across the street from the barbershop and waited for Esco. He gazed out his passenger window and admired the memorial that was made in the memory of Mills. Teddy bears, balloons, flowers and liquor bottles were lined up against the brick wall of the barbershop. Mills' eyes in a picture on a white tee shirt, stared back at him seeming to plea for revenge.

After ten minutes of waiting, Gage watched Esco pull into the parking space in front of him and hop out his car carrying a gym bag. He strolled to Gage's car and got in.

"It's a sawed off shotgun, a M-16, and an 11 shot nine in there," Esco said after he tossed the gym bag in the backseat. "Bullets too. That should be enough for you to hold ya spot down in case Flip or one of his young boys show they face."

Gage slapped hands with Esco then gave him a firm handshake.

"Good looking."

"That ain't about nothing. What's good though? How the fuck that nigga manage to get at Sharron? Niggas was posted all around the Masjid looking out for that nigga."

"Ya guess as good as mine. That shit's fucked up though. She ain't even have nothing to do with this shit."

"I feel you," Esco said, then paused. "Yo, Gage, I know you said you wasn't trying to get at Flip's bitch and all that, but I say we return the favor. That nigga must think shit's sweet doing shit like that."

Gage looked over at Esco then past him. His eyes locked with

As Dirty As It Gets

Mills' for the second time. Again Mills seemed to beg for revenge.

"Alright," Gage finally said. "What's the plan?"

"You know where that nigga's spot at down Atlanta right?"

"Yeah, I memorized the address from writing so much."

"Good. We gonna hit that nigga hard. Lil Kenny plugged us in with his bitch named Cream that work at Night on Broad. She knows Flip. She said he's supposed to go to the club tonight to check one of her girls. Clark and them gonna handle that while me and you catch a flight down ATL. I'ma get us some fake ID's and a couple plane tickets from my white boy. We should be on the plane tonight."

"If you already got the line on Flip what's the point in killing Monica?"

"Just cause we got the line don't mean shit's gonna go through. Nigga might not even show up. We hit her, we knock him off balance if this other shit don't go through, feel me?"

"I guess, but how we gonna get guns on a plane?"

"Fuck a gun. When we touch down in ATL we gonna buy a knife. I'ma fillet that bitch.

chapter

Thirteen

Clark snapped his phone shut then shifted in the front passenger seat so he could face Reef who was seated in the back. "That was the bitch Cream. She said that nigga in there right now. You ready?"

Reef screwed a silencer onto his machine gun then loaded a bullet into its chamber. "Let's go," he said.

Clark looked at his watch, it was a little after one in the morning. He looked over at Beefy who was behind the wheel of the Dodge Intrepid. "Pull up in three minutes."

Clark swung the car door open and stepped out. Reef was right behind him. The streets were dark and the traffic low. A light but steady rain created a fog like mist in the cold air. The two hit men tucked their weapons underneath the multi-colored designer hoodies they wore then crept around the corner to the club. A bouncer wearing a black jacket with the word "Security" stenciled across the front stood at the club's entrance. Clark approached him with a friendly smile. When the bouncer reached out to pat him down, Clark pulled out his gun and jammed it into the man's rib cage.

"Don't say shit unless you prepared to die," Clark said through gritted teeth. He gripped the bouncer by the collar of his jacket and forced him to turn around and walk through the front door.

Inside there was a long stairwell that lead downstairs to a pay booth and the club. Two more bouncers stood in front of the pay booth talking and a third was climbing the stairs towards the front door. Clark shoved his gun into the back of the bouncer he was holding at gunpoint and pulled the trigger. The power of the gun

As Dirty As It Gets

energized Clark. He kicked the bouncer in his ass, causing him to tumble down the steps into his co-worker. Before the other bouncers could react, Clark squeezed the trigger again. A swarm of bullets shot from the machine gun and riddled their bodies. Clark and Reef proceeded down the stairs and stepped over the dead bouncers on their way into the heart of the club.

After four shots of Remy V.S.O.P, Flip was loose. He sat on the couch in the middle of the club with Cream grinding her naked ass on his lap. It was his second dance with her and he flirted with the thought of taking her to a hotel.

Flip's thoughts were interrupted by sudden commotion coming from the bar area. He looked up in time to see the flash of gunfire and quickly held Cream in front of him as a shield. Bullets ripped into her back and knocked them both over the couch and onto the floor. Flip pushed Cream's dead body off of him then pulled his 40 cal. from his waistband. He peaked over the top of the couch and spotted two men shooting at him. He ducked back down and fired a few rounds from his hiding spot.

Out of the corner of his eye, Flip saw Pee-Wee and Noble side by side shooting back at the two men. That gave him a sense of hope. He stood up with his gun blazing and spotted one of the gunmen, shot in the leg, hobbling back towards the bar for cover.

The other gunman continued to fire. His bullets seemed endless but Flip's ten shot clip was empty in a matter of seconds.

Flip's hope to win the gun battle deflated when he saw Noble's light colored shirt explode into blotches of crimson. The gun Noble held slipped from his grasp and he clutched his neck. Blood shot from between his fingers before he fell face down on the floor.

Pee-Wee dropped next.

Flip screamed out in pain when a bullet grazed his forehead. More bullets slammed into the chest plate of his bulletproof vest. Out-numbered and out gunned, Flip did the only thing he could. Play dead.

chapter Fourteen

Flip sat in the backseat of the taxi exhausted. The past three days had been hectic. Losing Noble and almost getting killed weighed a little heavier on his shoulders than he anticipated. When he added the tension looming in the air every time he was around Pee-Wee and his young boys, he saw that he needed to regroup. The ongoing beef seemed to be eating away at his team's confidence in him, and that was not an option. He needed to fix the problem fast, so he decided to fly home where he could think clearly and put together a plan.

When the taxi stopped in front of his house, he smiled for the first time since the incident at Night on Broad. Monica's car was parked in its usual place next to his truck. He half expected for her car to be gone. She hadn't answered or returned his phone calls in days. Their last conversation was about her growing tired of him constantly running the streets. She told him if he didn't stop she'd leave, so not hearing from her made him think she made good on her threat.

After over paying the cabbie, Flip swung the cab's door open and stepped out holding two dozen pink roses, Monica's favorite. He planned to do a lot of sucking up and relieving the stress of war by having sex with the only woman he ever loved.

He strolled to his front door with a bop in his step. When he opened the door his world stopped. The pungent odor of death knocked the wind out of him. He dropped the roses and slowly walked into his home. He spotted Monica's body lying underneath a pool of dried up blood. His heart shattered into a million pieces that would never mend. Before he could catch himself, he collapsed to his knees and cried. His already hard heart hardened even more. With Monica gone, his only purpose for living was to kill.

chapter
Fifth teen

"This is the last time," Sinnamon said to herself. She was seated on the toilet in her bathroom rolling up a dollar bill. A mirror, with three lines of cocaine on it, sat on her lap. Her addiction held a stronger hold on her than she was willing to admit. This was her third "last time" getting high since she found out she was pregnant. She held the mirror up to her nose then used the dollar to snort two of the three lines. She put her head back and enjoyed the feeling. Once again she was temporarily relieved of her problems.

"Shhhh." She put her pointer finger to her lips thinking she heard something. A minute went by with her keeping still in an attempt to avoid making any noise.

"I'm bugging," she said when she didn't hear anything else. She brought the mirror back up to her nose and prepared to snort the last line. Suddenly the bathroom door swung open, causing her to jump. She dropped the mirror on her lap then looked towards the open door.

Esco stared at her with a murderous look on his face. She was caught red-handed.

"Let me explain," she managed to say.

Before she could stand, Esco was hovering over top of her. He snatched her by her neck and lifted her from the toilet. The mirror fell to the floor and shattered. She tried to pry his fingers from around her throat but failed.

"You wanna get high," Esco barked. "You gonna do it out in the streets with the rest of the junkies." He threw Sinnamon out of the bathroom. She fell onto their bedroom floor gasping for air. "Baby— please— let me explain," Sinnamon struggled to say.

As Dirty As It Gets

She looked up into Esco's eyes hoping to see signs of sympathy. There was none.

"I ain't trying to hear that shit," he said, as he grabbed her by her tee-shirt and dragged her towards the bedroom door. "Explain it to somebody on the street 'cause you getting the fuck outta my house."

"Please don't put me out," Sinnamon cried. "I promise I won't do it anymore." She tried to break away from Esco's hold, but it was no use. He dragged her out of the bedroom then down the stairs.

Esco stopped at the front door and opened it.

Sinnamon grabbed a hold of the doorframe and hung on to it as tight as she could.

He yanked her shirt hard, ripping it in the process. Her bare breast popped out from the ripped and stretched out cotton. He swatted her hands from the doorframe then shoved her once more. She fell to her knees on the cold ground then heard the front door slam shut and the lock click.

She looked at the door and couldn't believe the man who promised to marry her kicked her out in the cold wearing nothing but a tee shirt and a pair of extra-short shorts. She didn't even have shoes on her feet. She crawled to the welcome home mat that was at the base of the front door and sat on it with her knees to her chest. The cold air beat against her skin. Goose bumps covered her body and she shivered. She hugged her skinned knees and adjusted her tattered shirt to cover as much of her body as she could.

Esco sat on the other side of the door with his back against it. He massaged his temples wondering if he was wrong for putting Sinnamon out. The love he felt for her was the truest he'd experienced, but how could he have a junky for a wife.

"How could you do this to me," he heard her cry out. She banged on the door. "You open this door, damn it. This is my house too."

The banging grew louder.

"How can you turn your back on me when I need you the most? You said you loved me."

Esco didn't reply.

71

"Answer me, damn it." She banged on the door again. "I need you."

Sinnamon's cries began to wear Esco down.

"Ira please let me in, its cold and I'm pregnant. I don't want to get sick."

"Pregnant," Esco repeated the word like it was foreign. The sympathy he felt evaporated from the heat of his rising anger. He stood to his feet and opened the door. Sinnamon stood before him rubbing her shoulders. She tried to walk in the house but he placed his hand firmly on her chest and glared into her watering eyes.

"I'ma say this one time and one time only," he said. "You keep that shit up, we through and I promise you if something happens to my baby I'ma kill you."

CHaPTer SiXTeen

"If you just listen for a second, you'd understand why we should follow her," Detective Johnson said, sitting at his desk in his small office inside the Wilmington Police Station.

Detective Burton paced in front of the desk with his hands shoved in his pockets. "I'm not wasting my time following behind some girl. If anything we should follow her boyfriend."

"Not when everything revolves around the girl."

"Why— a couple of her friends were killed? That doesn't link her to the other murders."

Johnson cracked a smile then shuffled through a stack of papers that were on his desk. He slid a picture of Sharron's body out of the stack and passed it to Burton.

"I went to her funeral," Detective Johnson said.

"So."

"I saw Sinnamon and her boyfriend there with Anthony Parker."

"Who the hell is that?"

"Remember Sharron's husband, Marcus, the stiff that was found on Twenty-third Street?"

"Yeah."

"His partner, Gage."

"What the hell does that have to do with Sinnamon?"

Johnson picked up another stack of papers and flipped through them until he found what he was looking for: Ms. Jones's, Essence's and Shaquan's files. He passed Burton Essence's file first

"I'm sure you remember this lovely woman. Sinnamon's best friend according to the few people I questioned." Johnson now handed Burton Ms. Jones's file. "Sinnamon's neighbor and finally—" he stuck out Shaquan's kidnapping report. "Sinnamon's baby brother. Kidnapped the night Essence and the old woman was killed but returned shortly after according to the report."

Detective Burton looked puzzled. "What are you getting at?"

"What do all the vics have in common?"

"I don't know but I'm sure you're going to tell me."

"Sinnamon. She's connected to all of them. She was at Sharron's funeral, so she probably knew Marcus as well. The other three are obvious."

"Come on, you gotta give me more than that for me to believe a woman has something to do with all those murders."

"I'm not exactly labeling her a murderer. Although, I can't help but wonder if she was with Essence when she killed that guy. She may have even had something to do with our witness getting beaten to death."

"So if she's not a suspect, what are you getting at?" Burton asked.

"I think someone's after her. One of the witnesses to the shooting that took place after Essence's funeral said that the gunman was aiming for Sinnamon. They said Ira knocked her out the way. Once you add that to the fact that her little brother was kidnapped, it's obvious someone's after her. Why? I'm not sure, so don't ask. But my gut's telling me she pissed the wrong people off."

"I know this may seem like a shot in the dark but you have to admit, it does make sense and being that we don't have any suspect's why not keep tabs on the next possible victim?"

"Okay, I'll make a deal with you," Burton said. "I'll agree to follow Sinnamon for a week, and only a week, if you agree to tail Ira if we don't get anywhere with her. Agreed?"

Detective Johnson, grinning, reached across his desk and shook his partner's hand. "Agreed."

chapter seventeen

Gage sat down on one of the flat benches in the YMCA's gym and looked over at Esco who was a few feet away curling a pair of steel dumbbells. "So what are y'all hoping to have?" Gage asked.

"I don't really care what it is," Esco said. "I just pray it comes out healthy."

"Why you say it like that?"

Esco dropped the dumbbells on the rubber mat then sat down on an empty incline bench and stared at Gage for a moment.

"Between me and you," Esco said, "I caught her getting high."

"Sinnamon?"

"She was in our bathroom sniffing coke. Shit was crazy. I was so mad I drug her ass to the front door and put her out. I can't be fucking with no junkie. I'm thinking about making her get an abortion and cutting her off."

"That's foul, Es."

Esco scowled. "How the fuck is that foul? Bitch shouldn't be getting high, especially knowing she's pregnant."

Gage thought for a moment.

"That's your fiancée, right?" Gage said.

"Ya point?"

"All I'm saying is you obviously love her, and since you love her you need to be there for her."

Esco shook his head from side to side. "I can't be with no junkie."

"It's not about you Es. It's about her and that baby she's carrying."

Esco cast his eyes down like a scolded child and stared at the black rubber mat. "Fuck her."

"You don't feel like that so ain't no point in lying to yourself. If you love her like I know you do, you need to hold her down. This is when it counts the most. If you can't be there when someone's at rock bottom you don't really love them."

When Esco didn't respond Gage pried a bit.

"You do love her right?"

Esco looked up at Gage. "More than I want to. I ain't never feel this way about nobody before. I don't even know what to do right now."

"For starters y'all should make a doctor's appointment to make sure that baby alright."

"We did already. I'm taking her to that spot up there by Warner the day after tomorrow." Esco stood up. "You ready? Talking to you got me feeling all guilty and shit. I need to go holla at Sinnamon and get some things straight."

Gage looked at his watch. "Damn, I should've been home. I was supposed to meet Arrissa at the house before she got back from the grocery store. She's going to be spazzing if she beat me home."

Esco chuckled. "That's the part of the married life I ain't looking forward to."

The pair headed to the gym's locker room to gather the rest of their things. When they were done they strolled out of the YMCA and into the parking lot where their cars were parked side by side. They shook hands and pulled each other in for a brotherly hug.

"Make sure you make the right decision," Gage said when they broke their embrace.

"I am."

Gage got into his car and headed home. The highway was mostly empty, giving him the feeling of peace. It reminded him of his days in solitary confinement when he was alone in a six by nine cell with only his thoughts for company. In those days, he often dreamed of how things would be if he were granted his freedom again. He pictured himself the average square, working a nine to five or possibly investing his money in stocks or a business of his own. Crime and prison would be nothing more than faded memories. But now as a free man, his dreams had become nightmares.

He pulled up to his house and noticed Arrissa's Infinity in the driveway. The trunk was open, a prelude of the argument to come. He knew how much his wife hated hauling the grocery bags in the house.

"She just can't be patient," he mumbled as he parked alongside of his wife's car. He turned his engine off then got out and made his way to the Infinity's open trunk. Several plastic bags sat inside. He grabbed them all, and made his way to the front door hoping it was open because the bags were a lot heavier than he thought they'd be.

He tried the front door's handle and it didn't budge. "Damn," he said, then kicked the bottom of the door several times.

Arrissa didn't respond.

He took a few steps back and peered into the bay window at the front of the house. Only the lights in the kitchen were on.

"She plays too many games." He sat the bags down and removed his keys from his pocket then opened the door. "I know you heard me banging on the door," he yelled into the doorway. He picked up the bags and went into the house, kicking the door shut behind him.

Again, Arrissa didn't respond.

"Don't get an attitude with me cuz you hardheaded," Gage said, walking towards the kitchen. "I told you I'd take the bags in when I got back."

To Gage's surprise the kitchen was empty. He sat the bags down on the floor then hurried back toward the front of the house, turning on all of the lights. He had a bad feeling.

"Arrissa!" he called out. "Arrissa!" Still Arrissa didn't respond.

Gage rushed up the stairs and burst into their bedroom. She wasn't there.

He checked Hakim's room, all three of the guest rooms and both bathrooms.

Still no Arrissa.

The ringing of his cell phone distracted Gage away from his search. He hurriedly dug the phone out of his sweatpants.

"Arrissa?" he answered.

"G-G-Gage," Arrissa said into the phone before she burst out crying.

"Baby what's wrong? Where you at?"

Flip's voice suddenly hissed through the phone. "That doesn't matter right now."

"Where the fuck is my wife?"

"I need ya help."

"What the fuck, you ain't hear me? I said where the fuck is my wife?"

"Listen, I don't think that's the tone you want to use with me right about now. I mean, I do have ya wife and shit. Now like I said, I need ya help."

Gage did his best to calm himself. "Help with what?" he asked through gritted teeth.

"I need to find Esco and his bitch. I'm tired of looking for them. Give me an address or something."

"Why you putting me and my wife between y'all shit?"

"Leverage."

"By Allah, you hurt her I'ma—"

"Listen," Flip cut in. "Ain't nobody touch ya wife, at least not yet. If you want to keep it that way, you know what I want. Now you got ya options. Get at me when you choose.

The phone went dead.

chapter eighteen

Sinnamon's days of being called a 'junkie bitch' were over. She refused to take another minute of Esco's disrespect. Tonight it would all end. Her and Shaquan's bags were packed and sitting at the front door. She stood in the middle of her and Esco's room wearing a black leather jacket and gloves as she scanned the area for anything she may have forgotten. Nothing was in sight, but she did remember something.

She walked over to Esco's side of the bed and lifted the top part of the mattress. A black nine-millimeter handgun stared back at her. She grabbed it and felt a surge of energy. Her heart pounded with excitement but settled after a few seconds. She slipped the gun in the side pocket of her jacket then marched her way to the bedroom's door. With her hand on the door's knob she looked back. Her eyes rested on the large picture of her and Esco that hung over top of their bed. Tears began to flow.

"Come on Shaquan," she called out to her brother.

Shaquan walked out his room bundled in his winter coat, clutching a PSP in his hands. He looked from the game's screen to his sister.

"Why are you crying?" he asked in a soft voice.

Sinnamon wiped her tears and tried to muster a smile.

Shaquan walked over to her and hugged her waist. He looked up into Sinnamon's eyes and said, "It's okay, don't cry."

Sinnamon cried harder.

Once again it would be her and her baby brother facing the world alone. At least this time she had money. Life wouldn't be nearly as rough as it was before.

WASIIM

With Shaquan in tow, Sinnamon dragged herself down the steps and towards the front door, her strength to leave fading with every step, but she continued to move forward. When she reached the foyer, the front door swung open and Esco walked in.

Sinnamon froze. The little strength she gathered slipped, and again her tears flowed.

Esco placed his hand softly on the side of her face and tried to wipe her tears. She snatched out of his reach and batted his hand away.

"Don't touch me, Ira," she said evenly. "I'm done. I can't take any more of your abuse."

"Abuse? I ain't never put my hands on you."

"You beat me down with your words *every day,* Ira."

Sinnamon grabbed Shaquan by his hand, then grabbed the handle of one of the four suitcases she'd packed, and tried to ease out of the door. Esco stuck his arm out, blocking her path.

"I'm sorry," he said.

"Please, just get out my way and let me leave."

"We can't walk out on each other like this."

Sinnamon was tempted to pull the gun from her coat pocket. She couldn't believe Esco had the nerve to say that.

"Walk out on each other? Ira, you left me high and dry. When I needed you the most you tossed me, half naked and all, out of that door right there," she pointed behind Esco to the front door, "and told me to go live amongst the junkies. Fuck you."

"I'm not letting you walk out that door, now I said I was sorry."

"So I'm supposed to forgive you just like that?"

Esco took two steps forward and closed the space between them. Sinnamon wanted to back away but her feet remained planted on the floor. She looked Esco in his eyes and saw the flames of love.

"Yes, Sinnamon, just like that."

chapter nineteen

Gage's fist slammed into Monica's jaw. She crumpled to the floor unconscious at Esco's feet. Gage backed away, regretting what he knew was about to happen next.

Esco pulled a six-inch hunting knife from his back pocket then knelt beside the small woman. He grabbed a fist full of her hair and yanked her head back. In one swift motion he raked the blade across her throat. Then he vanished.

Monica's blood flowed like a fountain.

Gage tried to walk away but felt paralyzed. A force he had no strength to fight made him stand there and watch Monica bleed to death for reasons she'd never know.

She looked up at him with dead, haunting eyes. A smile eased across her face then she let out a sickly laugh. She clawed at her face, peeling away the skin until her face was no longer her own. Gage couldn't believe his eyes. He stumbled backwards, astonished that he was now staring at his wife.

"You killed me!" Arrissa screamed.

Gage jerked awake, gasping for air, his heart pounding in his chest. Sweat collected around his temples and the t-shirt he wore was drenched. He looked around and realized he was laying on the couch in his living room. He sat up and attempted to shake his nightmare but couldn't. The reminder of what he'd done was too vivid.

He grabbed his cell phone from the coffee table in front of the couch and dialed Flip for what seemed like the hundredth time. Again, the call went to a voicemail system that was full. He snapped his phone shut then sank back down onto the couch.

Stress was slowly eroding his sanity. Something needed to be done. Arrissa couldn't die.

With that thought in mind, Gage called the answer to his problems, Esco. After a brief conversation he was told to go to the Safari, a small bar in Wilmington.

Gage prepared himself for the task at hand. He dressed in a dark pair of jeans, a black thermal shirt and black Timberland boots. Once dressed, he went into his closet and retrieved a 9mm handgun that was inside a shoebox on the closet's shelf. It was one of the guns Esco had given him the day Sharron was murdered.

The gun felt perfect in his hands. It was cold and hard, just like he needed his heart to be to carry out tonight's plan. He popped the magazine from the gun. It was filled with hollow point bullets. He shoved the magazine back in its place then loaded a bullet into the gun's chamber.

He was getting his wife back. Tonight.

Gage turned onto the block the Safari was located in time to see Esco parking up the street from the bar. Perfect. Now all he had to do was find a place to park. He had to move fast if things were going to go as planned. He found an empty parking space on a narrow street around the corner from the Safari. He parked, then got out of his car and hustled around the corner. The nine was secured in his waistband. He reached under his thermal and gripped the butt of the gun as he bent the corner. *A couple shots and it's all over.* He'd flee back to his car, hop in and make a clean get away.

"Damn," he said, disappointed that Esco was already walking into the Safari. He released his grip on the nine and strolled casually to the bar's door. Hopefully another opportunity would present itself before the end of the night.

Inside the Safari, Gage spotted Esco seated on a barstool at the bar. Gage eased onto the stool next to Esco and greeted him with a handshake and brotherly hug.

"So what got the married man at the bar—" Esco looked at his watch, "at eleven o'clock at night?"

"The missus beefing," Gage answered.

"You know you making that marriage shit seemed fucked up right?"

As Dirty As It Gets

Gage faked a laugh. "Yeah, the married life."

"So what you drinking? It's on me."

"Get me whatever you getting."

Esco waved a bartender over. The shapely woman leaned on the bar in front of Gage and Esco, giving them an eye full of her cleavage. "What can I get you?" she asked.

"Two double shots of Remy V.S.O.P and two Heinekens," Esco said.

The bartender spun around to get their drinks.

"So what's good with you and Sinnamon? Everything cool?" Gage asked.

Esco smiled. "Yeah. We talked and everything's back to normal."

"That's what's up. Y'all still going to that doctor's appointment?"

"Yeah. Hopefully everything's cool with the baby, but enough of that, what's up with you? You look stress."

The bartender sat the drinks in front of them. Esco passed her a fifty and told her to keep the change. She thanked him then went on her way.

"What's ya wife beefing about?" Esco asked.

"She got an idea of what's going on, said I should just let shit be."

"And she ain't saying nothing wrong. You fresh out of jail wit a wife and a son. You supposed to be past that street shit."

"I couldn't just let Flip do all he did and not do something about it. I ain't never been a sucker."

"It ain't about being a sucker, Gage. Once you made the decision to change it was about being true to ya'self and ya family, not to mention ya religion." Esco took a gulp of his beer.

"To keep it one hundred," Esco said, "now that Sinnamon's pregnant and we about to get married, I'm leaving the streets behind and never looking back. I'ma focus on my music and invest some of that money I made with a uncle I got that lives in Jamaica."

"That's what's up, you thinking like that," Gage said. "But what you going to do about this situation with Flip?"

WASIIM

"Ain't no need to worry about a corpse."

Gage wasn't sure if he should tell Esco that Flip wasn't dead. A few seconds of silence passed before Gage decided that it wouldn't hurt to let Esco know that Flip wasn't exactly a corpse.

"Flip ain't dead," Gage said, then downed his Remy in one swallow.

"What the fuck you talking about? Niggas handled him the same night we went down Atlanta."

"Well, shit must've went wrong cuz Flip called me yesterday."

Fire flickered in Esco's eyes. "And you just now telling me?"

Gage dropped his right hand on his lap so he could draw his gun if things went sour. The man peering into his eyes was a killer just like him.

"I've been caught up in my own shit so I ain't have time—"

"Ain't have time? It only takes a couple seconds to make a phone call."

"I felt that was something we needed to talk about face to face." Gage was now the one peering into Esco's eyes, but Esco looked past him.

"You got ya gun on you?" Esco asked.

Gage instinctively reached under his shirt. "Yeah, why? What's up?"

Esco nodded his head towards the entrance of the bar.

Gage turned to look and saw a man with a big scar on his cheek standing by the door talking on a cell phone.

"I gave him that scar last summer at a dice game," Esco said.

"What you want to do?"

Esco stood up. "I ain't trying to get you caught up in no more of my shit so let's try to slip out of here. Besides, I don't want to kill that nigga, not in here anyway."

Gage got up and followed Esco to the door. Scarface didn't even look in their direction when they walked by. Gage began to wonder if Esco was lying about slashing the man's face. Maybe Esco's beef wasn't with the man at all, maybe it was him Esco didn't want to kill in the bar. They were outside now walking up an almost empty street. Anything was possible. Gage gripped the butt of the nine. He came to ensure his wife's safety, not die.

84

As Dirty As It Gets

"Ain't no need to run now," a voice came from behind them.

Gage and Esco both spun around. Scarface was pointing a large handgun in their direction.

The first shot echoed.

The few passerbies sprinted away like track stars.

Gage and Esco took shelter behind two separate cars, pulled their guns and returned fire.

A dark colored Buick came speeding up the street. It skidded to a stop right where the shootout was taking place. Gage thought cops and jail until two young looking black men jumped out the car with guns blazing.

Gage fired at them, hitting one of the men in the abdomen. The man fell to his knees, clutching his stomach and dropped his gun. The other gunman ran to the other side of the Buick and sent a barrage of bullets from a machine gun in Gage's direction.

The rear window of the late model Taurus Gage was squatted behind, shattered and bullets drummed against the body of the car. Gage wondered if the drum roll would ever stop. He fired a few more rounds then heard an unwanted click of metal.

His nine was out of bullets.

"Shit," Gage said, sinking back behind the Taurus. He spotted Esco trying to gun down Scarface. "Es cover me," Gage yelled.

Esco fired a few rounds towards the Buick then pulled a revolver from his waistband and tossed it to Gage.

Gage snatched the gun out of the air then peeked through the windows of the bullet riddled Taurus. He spotted Machine Gun creeping in his direction. The man either misjudged the situation or had balls the size of an elephant's because he was walking unprotected in the middle of the street while bullets were flying.

From behind the safety of the Taurus, Gage fired three quick rounds. He heard a low moan then the sound of metal hitting concrete. Machine gun was down.

Gage glanced in Esco's direction. Esco's back was towards him. This was the moment he'd been waiting for. He didn't want to do it, but did he have a choice?

Not with his wife's life on the line.

He lifted his gun and aimed at Esco's head. Perfect opportunity.

WASIIM

Perfect shot. He took a deep breath.

The smoke was about to clear.

A spray of bullets slammed into the Taurus, jarring Gage from his focus. Another window shattered. More bullets burst in the air then the faint screams of sirens could be heard.

"The cops coming," Gage yelled. The sirens screamed louder.

Machine gun let out another stream of bullets. Gage fired back two shots then the gun clicked. No more bullets again.

It was time to get out of there. Everyone must've had the same thought because Machine gun hobbled back to the Buick and jumped in. Scarface followed behind him. The third gunman was left in the street to die. His friends did nothing to help him.

The Buick peeled off fast and almost hit an approaching cop car, a plus for Gage and Esco. They had more time to escape now be-cause the police gave chase to the Buick.

"Call me and let me know you made it home safe," Esco said before he and Gage parted ways.

Gage jogged back towards his car. He used his thermal to wipe his prints off his guns then tossed them in the trashcan in an alley-way before he got into his car and pulled off.

That was a close call. Too close.

Gage's thoughts shifted to his wife. He failed her, that much was obvious, but he wasn't giving up. He already had another plan. Letting his wife die was not an option.

chapter Twenty

Flip looked at his cell phone as it rung. Gage's name flashed across the screen for the fifth time in a row. He took a deep drag from a cigarette drenched in PCP then blew smoke at the phone. Laughing like a madman, Flip laid back in his recliner and pressed the button to decline Gage's call. The longer he let Gage sweat, the better he knew his results would be.

"Ya husband blowing up my phone is starting to get on my fucking nerves," Flip said.

Arrissa sat on a couch on the other side of the room. Despite one of her wrist being handcuffed to the radiator that was next to the couch, she looked comfortable. Pillows were placed all around the bourgeois prisoner, and the TV was on exactly what she want-ed to watch.

"What do you expect," Arrissa said, looking from the TV to Flip. "You need to just let me go."

"No, I need to get Esco and that bitch."

"Well, how do you expect to get them if you keep ignoring Gage's calls? I'm sure he has something for you by now."

"You might be right, but I'ma make that nigga sweat a little longer. I wanna make sure he tells me something I wanna hear."

"Well you need to stop playing games and answer the damn phone the next time he calls." Arrissa rolled her eyes. "And stop smoking that stinking shit. You're crazy enough as it is."

Flip took another drag from the PCP laced cigarette. The fire was near the filter now. He flicked the cigarette butt, still burning, across the room. It landed on Arrissa's over garment. She jumped up from the couch and tried to get the burning cigarette butt off of her, a tough job being that she was handcuffed. However, she succeeded then sat back down. The look she gave Flip showed every bit of the hate she had for him.

Flip blew a cloud of smoke in Arrissa's direction and laughed. He grabbed another PCP drenched cigarette and a lighter from the table that was next to his recliner. He put the cigarette between his lips and lit it.

The ringing of Flip's phone sliced through the tension in the room. He looked at the phone's screen. Gage was calling again. This time he decided to answer the call.

"Did you decide what you wanted to do yet?" Flip said into the phone.

"Let me speak to my wife."

Flip got up from the recliner and walked over to Arrissa. She watched him with hate-filled eyes as he sat next to her on the couch. "You got one minute," Flip said, passing Arrissa his cell phone.

"Hello?" Arrissa said into the receiver. Half of a smile eased across her face as she listened to Gage talk.

"Yeah, I'm fine," she told her husband. "I'm just ready to come home." She listened some more then said, "Everything's been cool. He's just waiting for you to tell him what he wants to know." A look of concern crossed her face for a moment. "You are going to tell him right?" The smile on Arrissa's face told Flip everything he needed to know.

"I love—" Flip snatched the phone from her.

"Let's get down to business," Flip said.

Chapter
Twenty one

Sinnamon stood in front of the floor length mirror in her bedroom. A smile beamed across her face. She was one sexy mom. The peek of cleavage her expensive blouse revealed looked inviting and her skinny jeans hugged every curve. She turned her feet sideways, one at a time, to check out her four-inch ankle boots and just as she figured, they looked damn good on her too.

She strutted into her walk-in closet. Her extensive collection of high-end pocketbooks and handbags hung on little hooks on the closets back wall. She chose a small brown clutch, one out of the two she bought to match the ankle boots she was wearing, then stepped out of the closet. It was time to hit the road.

She slipped on a waist length, brown leather jacket then looked at her watch. It was 10:40 a.m., which meant she had twenty minutes to get to her prenatal appointment; plenty of time being that the doctor's office wasn't even a five-minute drive from her house.

On the way out of her bedroom, she grabbed the keys to her Bentley and her cell phone off her dresser. She tossed the phone in her clutch and was about to call out for Shaquan but remembered Esco's mother had picked him up the night before. It was hard to let her brother stay with someone else after his kidnapping, but Esco was right, she needed a break. And now that she had one, she intended to take full advantage of it. After the doctor's appointment, she planned to tear the mall down.

She deactivated the alarm to her car, got in and started the engine. The engine purred, and Mary J. Blige's classic hit "Real

Love" poured through the Bentley's speakers.

The song made Sinnamon think of Esco. His love for her was real. Not only did he agree to stick by her and help her through her drug problem, but he also said he was quitting the drug game. To-day was actually his last day dealing.

Sinnamon pulled out of her driveway singing along with Mary. After driving a few blocks, she noticed a Dodge Charger trailing her. It was the only car behind her and the driver seemed to be trying a little too hard to keep its distance.

She made a turn and seconds later the Charger was behind her again. She slowed down and tried to get a glimpse of the occupants inside the trailing car, but the glare on the Charger's windshield didn't allow her a clear look. However, she was able to make out two figures.

Sinnamon fumbled through her clutch for her cell phone. She found it and dialed Esco.

He answered on the second ring. "What's up babe?"

"I think somebody's following me," Sinnamon said, trying to sound calm.

"Where you at?"

"Almost at the doctor's office, what should I do?"

"Turn your radio off, then turn it back on, turn your heat all the way up, then turn the volume to two and put the radio station on 101.7."

Sinnamon did as she was told and after turning the radio to the right station, the driver's seat vibrated then she heard a muffled click. When the seat vibrated again, a small drawer slid out from underneath it, revealing a silver .380. She grabbed the little gun and loaded a bullet into its chamber.

"You do like I said?" Esco asked.

"Yeah, I got it. Now what do you want me to do?" "How far are you from the doctor's office?"

"I'm right up the street."

"That's good, keep coming this way, I'm not far from you. I want you to ride down Monkey Hill and stay on those back roads. We gonna get these niggas. I ain't going to let nothing happen to you."

"I know you're not, baby. I love you."

As Dirty As It Gets

Sinnamon pressed the button that activated her cell phones speaker so she could still communicate with Esco, then sat the phone in one of the Bentley's cup holders. She clutched the gun in her right hand and the steering wheel in her left.

"Oh my God," Sinnamon screamed. A late model Crown Vic was speeding towards her.

She swerved the Bentley to the left, barely avoiding a head-on collision, but the Crown Vic still slammed into the rear side of her car. The driver's side impact airbag exploded into Sinnamon's face, knocking the gun out of her hand, and causing the car to stall.

Dazed, Sinnamon peeked in her rearview mirror and saw that the Crown Vic had crashed head-on with the Charger. Good, now she could get away. She restarted the engine then slammed her foot down on the gas pedal. The Bentley's V-12 engine roared to life and it's tires screamed, but the car went nowhere.

Blood trickled from Flip's forehead down to his face. He wiped the blood with a gloved hand then removed the .45 from his shoulder holster and thumbed the guns safety off. A grin crept across his face when he noticed that the PCP soaked cigarette he put in the ashtray before the crash was still there and lit. He snatched the cigarette out of the ashtray and took a deep drag.

High was an understatement. The way Flip, felt he could kiss the moon.

"You's a dumb mutha-fucka."

Flip had forgotten about his passenger. He looked to his right and Pee-Wee, bleeding from his nose, glared back at him. The large man struggled to free himself from his seatbelt and looked pissed. Flip offered him the cigarette.

"Do I look like I want to smoke that shit," Pee-Wee said, smacking the cigarette out of Flip's hand. "You could've killed us."

Flip's eyes went from Pee-Wee to his precious cigarette, that was now unlit and stuck between the center console and driver's seat, then back to Pee-Wee. "You shouldn't have did that," Flip said calmly.

"I don't give—"

Flip pressed the barrel of the .45 against Pee-Wee's forehead and pulled the trigger. The pistol's blast drowned out what was left of Pee-Wee's disrespect and blew his brains all over the passenger side of the car.

Flip reached across the center console and lifted up Pee-Wee's shirt. The large handle of a black gun stuck out from his dead friend's waistline. He removed the gun and looked it over. The words *.50 Caliber Dessert Eagle* were engraved on the side of the barrel. He checked to see if the gun's safety was on. It wasn't, and the hammer was already cocked back. The gun was ready to be fired.

He swung the driver's door open then stepped out gripping the .45 in his right hand and the Dessert Eagle in his left. His eyes were locked on the Bentley. Sinnamon was going to die today.

"Police," someone shouted to his right. "Freeze."

He whipped his head in the direction the voice came from and locked eyes with a bearded man who was standing just outside the passenger door of the totaled Charger. The man was definitely part of the Wilmington PD. Both of his hands were wrapped firmly around a glock that was aimed at Flip's head and a silver badge hung from a thin chain that was around his neck.

This was not part of the plan, but a cop wasn't about to ruin Flip's date with Sinnamon.

He opened fire with the Dessert Eagle, the large gun kicking like a mule with each shot. Two bullets buried themselves in the cop's chest; another dug a hole in his forehead. The cop crumbled to the ground, dropping his gun.

Flip jumped onto the hood of the Crown Vic and fired both guns at the Bentley. Bullets ripped through the body of the car and shattered the back window. The driver's door of the Bentley swung open and another gun echoed. A bullet buzzed by Flip's ear. The bitch was shooting back.

Enraged, Flip worked the triggers of both guns faster. Sinnamon continued to fire back.

A bullet grazed Flip on his shoulder. He jumped off of the car and took cover behind it. Looking through the Crown Vic's windows he tried to get a good view of Sinnamon. He couldn't see her. She was no longer shooting, but she had to be hiding behind the Bentley.

He dropped to his knees, crouched down and looked under the Crown Vic to the Bentley. He couldn't remember the last time he saw a sight so sweet. Sinnamon was sprawled on the pavement bleeding.

He stood to his feet, a sense of victory pulsing through his veins. He couldn't wait to look into Sinnamon's eyes and put a bullet in her head. He maneuvered around the Crown Vic, both guns pointed in Sinnamon's direction.

A gunshot echoed.

Pain exploded in his bicep. He dropped the .45 and fell to his knees. He used the trunk of the Crown Vic to pull himself back up. His arm was throbbing, but he had to see who was shooting at him. They deserved to die, trying to save a bitch like Sinnamon.

Another cop was standing next to the Charger, his gun aimed at Flip. Flip ducked behind the Crown Vic just as the cop fired twice more, then he heard a walkie-talkie chirp and the cop yell for back up. His plans were falling apart and his high was blown. It wouldn't be long before there were a million cops in the area. He had to get away.

Or die trying.

He snatched the .45 up off the ground then sprinted as fast as he could towards the next street over while firing both guns at the cop. The barking guns kept the cop at bay, allowing Flip to escape. He found himself in a quiet neighborhood, it looked like the suburbs, but he knew he was in the city. He was familiar enough with Wilmington to know that he was near I-95, a route back to Philly, and his highway to freedom.

Sirens. He could hear them closing in.

He needed a car. There were plenty to choose from— if he had the keys to start them…or a screwdriver. He didn't know how to hot-wire a car.

A thin white man, at least sixty years old, stepped out of one of the houses. His gray mop of hair looked a mess on his head, and his face was stern, mad looking. He appeared to be having a bad day, if not, he was about to have one. A set of keys were in his wrinkled, liver spotted hands, and Flip wanted them bad.

WASIIM

He stalked the man up the block to a late model Benz. The old man didn't look back once. The neighborhood watch signs must've made him believe his quiet little block was safe. Maybe on a normal day it was, but today wasn't normal.

"Give me the fucking keys," Flip said, pushing the barrel of the .45 into the back of the old man's neck.

"I'll do no such thing." The old man turned around with his chest poked out and faced Flip. There wasn't a trace of fear on his pale face.

Flip admired the man's bravery for a split second then struck him over the top of his head with the Dessert Eagle. Mr. Brave Ass crumpled to the ground unconscious and dropped his keys in front of the car. Flip grabbed the keys then hustled to the Benz's trunk and opened it. He tucked the guns in his waistband then hustled back to the old man.

Blood was leaking from the old man's head, but he was still breathing. Flip hoisted him over his shoulder then took him to the trunk and stuffed him inside. He slammed the trunk shut then got into the car. The sirens were so loud by then he expected to see a cop car any second, so he pulled off slowly, trying his best not to draw any attention to himself.

chapter
Twenty Two

"That's my fiancée," Esco shouted at an unusually pale and pudgy uniformed cop that was blocking his path to Sinnamon. "This is a crime scene sir, and I can't let you disturb it," the cop said.

"That's my fucking fiancée they putting in that ambulance." Esco pointed behind the cop to Sinnamon who was being strapped into a gurney. Her clothes were soaked with blood and one of the two paramedics working on her was pumping air into her lungs with a CPR breathing apparatus.

"I don't care who it is," the pudgy cop said. "An officer was murdered and you or nobody else is going to compromise this scene."

Esco gripped the cop by the collar of his uniform. "Who the fuck you think you talking to."

"Calm down, Ira." Esco looked up in time to see Detective Johnson stepping in between him and the cop. The detective looked Esco in the eyes and placed a hand on his shoulder. "I'ma let you go with your girl, but you owe me."

"Whatever," Esco said before he brushed past the detective and jogged over to the lady paramedic that had just shut the backdoors of the ambulance truck. "That's my fiancée, can I ride with her?"

"I'm sorry, but that's not a good idea," the paramedic said, rushing to the driver's side of the truck. "They're working on her in the back and if we don't get her to Christiana Hospital soon, she might not make it."

Esco watched in defeat as the woman hopped into the truck and slammed the driver's door shut. The ambulance's lights flickered then the sirens blared. The truck sped off leaving Esco with a sinking feeling in his gut.

"I tried to help you," Detective Johnson said from behind him, "now can you please help me?"

Esco turned around and stood face to face with Detective Johnson. "No," Esco said.

"Come on, Ira, I know you know something. My partner was just murdered and it doesn't look like your fiancée is doing too much better. We can work together."

"I don't know nothing," Esco said, walking away.

Detective Johnson grabbed Esco by his shoulder and spun him around. "You're going to talk to me here and now." Spittle flew from the detective's mouth as he spoke. "Or that little bitch of yours will be charged with conspiracy to the murder of a police officer. If that doesn't stick, I'll see to it that she gets the max for the gun she had."

Esco pushed Detective Johnson away from him. "Don't ever touch or talk to me like that again."

"Okay, assault on an officer. That's fine by me. You're under arrest." Detective Johnson pulled out his cuffs.

"Fuck you," Esco said, then pushed the detective again, this time harder. A swarm of cops quickly came to Detective Johnson's aide. Together they wrestled Esco to the ground and subdued him.

"This is some bullshit," Esco yelled.

Detective Johnson put the cuffs tightly on his wrist. "No, you not knowing anything is bullshit," he said, breathing hard. "Maybe you'll sing another tune down at the station."

Chapter
Twenty Three

Tears flowed down Gage's face as he recited the opening verse of the Quran in the Arabic language. He was in the middle of offering the evening prayer for Muslims. The words of his Lord gripped and shook his soul to its core. He wanted desperately to stay on the straight path and avoid Allah's punishment, but the ways of the world continued to pull him in the wrong direction.

He prostrated for the final time, kept his face pressed against the rug, and begged Allah for the safe return of his wife. After praying, Gage looked to his right. His son was kneeling on his knees, imitating at him. He took Hakim in his arms and hugged him, then kissed him on his forehead.

"I love you," Gage said.

"I love you too, Dad."

The tranquility he felt from the prayer, along with the presence of his son, put Gage at ease for the moment. He and Hakim made their way over to the couch that sat in front of the large TV in the living room and sat down. Gage picked up the remote control and flipped through the channels until Sponge Bob popped on the screen. Knowing how much his son enjoyed the cartoon, Gage sat the remote control on the couch's armrest, then made himself comfortable.

In minutes the TV screen became a blur and the character's words no longer held any meaning. Gage's mind was on his wife. He missed her more than words could describe and her absence was taking a toll on him. Sleep was a distant memory and he was barely able to eat enough to keep his strength.

An hour passed before Gage looked over at Hakim and noticed

he was asleep. He got up from the couch and lifted his son in his arms and carried him upstairs to his bedroom. He pulled back the thick blue comforter on Hakim's racecar shaped bed, then carefully laid him down. He tucked Hakim in, then stepped back and looked down on his only child, his thoughts now on his own father. Would things be different if his father had played a part in his life? Would life have been as hard? He quickly shook the thought, knowing there was no such thing as "ifs". Everything he'd been through in life was by the decree of Allah and nobody had the power to change that.

In a barely audible voice, Gage told his son that he loved him, then headed back down to the living room. He plopped down on the couch and stared at the TV. Another cartoon was on. He grabbed the remote control then aimed it at the TV as if it was a gun and pressed the power button. The TV screen went blank and darkness swallowed everything in the room. The house became quiet and again thoughts of Arrissa invaded his mind.

The soft sound of footsteps jerked Gage out of his thoughts. He got up then lifted one of the cushions on the couch and grabbed the double barrel shotgun Esco had given him. He cocked the hammer back, then pointed the gun at the front door. His finger caressed the trigger as he waited.

A shadow passed by the front window, then keys jingled. Gage's heart began to pound. He gripped the gun tighter. Sweat collected on his forehead and around his eyebrows. The sound of the key entering the keyhole was like thunder. When the front door cracked open, the lights from outside spilled into the house. Gage's eyes settled on Arrissa and he sighed in relief. The weight of the world was finally lifted from his shoulders.

chapter Twenty Four

"You ready to talk yet?" Detective Johnson said, standing in front of the cell Esco was in.

Esco sat up on the metal bunk and glared at the detective through the steel bars of his cage. The sight of the detective made his blood boil. He'd been in the cold, uncomfortable cell for hours without so much as a phone call.

"We ain't got nothing to talk about," Esco said. "Just charge me with what you gonna charge me with, so I can see the judge."

"Actually, we got a lot to talk about." Detective Johnson removed a large set of keys from a clip that was attached to his belt then opened the cell door. "Get up and turn around, so I can cuff you."

The thought of protesting crossed Esco's mind but he figured it was pointless. The longer he prolonged things, the longer it'd be before he was out on bail and at the hospital with Sinnamon. He got up from the bunk and took a couple of steps toward Detective Johnson before turning around. It didn't surprise him when the detective put the cuffs on extra tight.

"Follow me," Detective Johnson said.

Esco followed the detective to an open elevator that they boarded and rode up one level. When the elevator stopped, they got off, and Esco followed the detective down a narrow hall.

Detective Johnson stopped at the first door, opened it and let Esco enter ahead of him.

"This doesn't have to take long," Detective Johnson said, following Esco into the room and shutting the door. "Turn around so I can take those cuffs off."

WASIIM

Esco turned around without objecting.

Detective Johnson took the cuffs off of Esco then pointed to a stool that was at the back of the room. "Have a seat."

Esco sat down and noticed a few folders on the table. Detective Johnson snatched one of Esco's hands then cuffed it to a steel hook that was bolted to the wall.

"There's been a lot of homicides in the city lately," the detective said.

Esco didn't respond.

Johnson picked up one of the folders and pulled out a thin stack of pictures. He began to pace around the small room. "I've been doing a lot of investigating too." He stopped next to Esco and stared down at him. "That's how I know you have something to do with all this."

Esco still didn't respond.

Detective Johnson slowly shuffled through the pictures one by one. "I'm sure you remember her," he said, placing a picture on the table.

Esco looked at the picture for a moment. It was of Essence at her murder scene. She was laid out on the blood stained couch in her living room with a small hole in her forehead. Her eyes and mouth were open in fear, a reminder of how unexpected death could be.

"Who did it?" Detective Johnson asked. Esco remained quiet.

The detective chuckled. "Is that why you did this?" He slammed a shot of Mills' body down on the table.

Esco didn't flinch.

"How about the rest of this shit?" Detective Johnson yelled, slamming the remaining four pictures on the table.

Esco looked at the pictures and only recognized Sharron and Mrs. Jones.

"You don't have to say anything, Ira," Detective Johnson said. "I know what's going on and believe me, somebody's going to be charged with every last one of these murders." The detective brought his face so close to Esco's that Esco could feel the heat of his breath. "I don't care if it takes me the rest of my life. Somebody's going down."

Chapter Twenty Five

Betty walked out of the building from her NA meeting and stood on the corner of Twenty-seventh and Washington. The world looked totally different. Six months ago she would've never noticed how bright the sun could be on a cold spring day or how fresh the air was. She looked down at the key chain she clutched in her hand and grinned like a child holding a new toy. She couldn't believe she'd been free from Lady Heroin for six months.

For ten long years she had been a prisoner to her addiction. Not even the love she had for her children had been strong enough to free her from the chains that were latched so tightly on her. It wasn't until she was arrested for drug possession and forced to spend sixty-seven days in prison that she decided to free herself.

Her first week in prison had been worse than death. The fact that her freedom was stripped away was minute compared to the withdrawal she went through. Her body ached night and day. She couldn't keep herself from throwing up or releasing her bowels; eating was a privilege she only experienced in her dreams, and her already malnutritioned frame was slowly withering away. Just when she thought God was going to bless her with the sweetness of death, he did her one better; he gave her another shot at life. When the worst of her withdrawal subsided, her thoughts became clearer than they had been in years. After attending her first NA meeting, she knew that she would never return to the life of a drug addict.

Betty strolled to her car, a dark blue '98 Honda Civic that she brought from an auction for $1,500. With her checks from her job at Pathmark, it took her three months to save up the money to purchase the car. It was worth every penny. The Civic was in pretty good condition and happened to be her favorite color.

As Betty was opening the car's door she was drawn to a conversation that two young girls were having as they walked by. She studied the girls for a moment. Their bodies, barely covered in extra tight clothing, screamed that they were mature adults, but their faces whispered the truth. They were barely teenagers.

"Yeah, Esco's girl," the shorter of the two was saying. "They shot her up when she was riding in her car."

The young girl's words paralyzed Betty for a moment.

"For real," the other girl said, twisting her neck in a ghetto fashion. "In that Bentley? Girl, that car was soooo hot. I'ma get me one when my baby comes up in the game."

"And is!" The shorter one slapped hands with her friend.

"So did the girl die?"

Betty waited anxiously for the answer.

"I don't know, my cousin ain't say." The rest of what the girl was saying faded as the distance grew between Betty and the two girls.

Betty got into her car and attempted to put the key in the ignition but couldn't. Her hands shook too much, causing her to miss the keyhole.

After the third attempt, she finally succeeded and started the car. She took a deep breath and pulled herself together. She had to make it to the hospital.

Betty rushed into Christiana Hospital and ran straight to the information desk where a Hispanic woman was seated in front of a computer typing. The woman smiled warmly when Betty approached the desk.

"Excuse me." Betty glanced at the woman's name tag. "Ms. Lopez, I hate to bother you, but I need to know if my daughter is here. Her name is Sinnamon Dupree. I was told she may have been shot."

"Hold on just a second." The receptionist rapidly struck the keyboard with her fingertips then clicked the mouse a few times. "Yes, she's here. She came in yesterday. They have her in ICU." Betty's heart sank and tears welled in her eyes.

As Dirty As It Gets

The receptionist wrote something on a small piece of paper then passed the paper to Betty. "That's the room number."

Betty looked at the numbers scribbled on the paper then headed towards the elevators. She didn't know what to expect once she got to her daughter's room. ICU in the nature that she pictured it was one step away from death. And if her daughter died, how could she ever apologize for all the pain she caused for not being a mother.

She rode the elevator up to the fourth floor alone, running away from her thoughts as she paced the small area the elevator had to offer. She jumped when the elevator's bell rang and its doors slid open. A short prayer rolled off her tongue when she stepped out into the hall and followed the numbered arrows that pointed to her daughter's room. Her heart drummed when she spotted two uniformed officers posted next to the door that was marked with the number 423, the same number that was scribbled on the piece of paper she held in her hand. She avoided eye contact with the officers and continued to walk to the room.

"Can I help you ma'am?"

Betty knew the extremely deep voice belonged to one of the officers and almost ran. She had to remind herself that she was a changed woman and wasn't doing anything wrong. She looked directly at the officers for the first time and realized they were both black; young and black. A feeling of ease washed over her and a smile spread across her face.

"I'm just visiting my daughter," Betty said.

"Not if you don't have ID." The lighter of the two officers said. The smile on Betty's face faded. She shoved her hand into her purse and fished out her wallet. She slid her I.D. out, then handed it to the police officer that asked about it. He took it and jotted her name down in a small notepad.

"Don't be long," the officer said, handing Betty back her I.D.

She snatched her I.D., pushed open the door that led to Sinnamon's room, and walked in. She froze at the sight of her first born lying helpless on the hospital bed. Tubes were jammed in her nose and an I.V. was hooked to her arm. A heart monitor beeped slow and steady, a complete contrast to Betty's racing heart.

WASIIM

Almost a full minute passed before Betty was able to force herself to move. She walked over to Sinnamon's bedside and stared at her daughter for a minute. Tears trickled down her cheeks. She grabbed Sinnamon's hand and noticed the silver handcuffs for the first time. Her baby girl was handcuffed to a bed as she fought for her life. Betty couldn't understand it.

The room's door cracked open. Betty turned around expecting to see one of the police officers that were posted outside the door. She sighed in relief when she spotted a slim woman in hospital scrubs. Dealing with the police officer's rudeness wasn't something she was in the mood for.

"Hi, I'm Shayla," the woman said, smiling. "I'm one of the surgical techs that helped with her surgery. I've been checking on her periodically. Everything seems to be going well. The worst is over."

"Thank you," Betty said, forcing a smile.

"Here you go." Shayla took a few tissues from her top pocket and handed them to Betty. "Is she your daughter?" Betty nodded.

Shayla put her hands on Betty's shoulders. "Everything's going to be okay. Your daughter is going to pull through, and the baby is perfectly fine."

"Baby?"

"You didn't know?"

This time Betty managed a genuine smile. "No, I didn't. How far along is she?"

"Almost two months. The baby's growth is excellent and despite the shooting, nothing is abnormal. The doctor said it's a miracle because the bullet that struck Sinnamon in her butt traveled up to her midsection but didn't cause any serious damage. The sergeant was able to remove it with ease. Your daughter's a tough woman. We have to monitor her here for a few more days, then she'll be moved to a regular room.

"Thanks for all of your help," Betty said, feeling a lot better. Just hearing that her daughter was going to pull through lifted her spirits, and the fact that Sinnamon was pregnant made things all the better. Maybe now she could help Sinnamon be the mother that she never was.

chapter Twenty six

Gage was in bed with his wife when his cell phone rang. "Hello," he answered.

"Yo Gage, this Esco, I need you to do me a favor."

Gage sat up in the bed. "What's good?"

"I'm down turnkey. I need somebody to post my bail. I can't reach my mom, so I was trying to see if you could get ya wife to do it."

Gage looked over at Arrissa knowing she wasn't going to be happy about the request.

"My bail only $50,000 secured. I'll give you the five stacks back later on today."

"I got you. We gonna shoot over to the bail bondsman now. You'll be out in a minute."

"Good looking. I'll holler at you when they let me out."

"Alright." Gage hung up the phone.

"Who was that?" Arrissa asked.

"Esco," Gage said, getting out of the bed.

Arrissa scowled. "I know you ain't just tell him that we're gonna bail him out."

"Listen, babe, we a team, so I really need you to ride with me on this."

"So you're gonna act like I didn't get kidnapped and everything else?"

Gage slipped into a pair of sweatpants. "Just get dressed so we can get this out of the way."

"No." Arrissa sat up and leaned back against the headboard

with her arms folded across her chest.

"Baby, why you gotta make things difficult? My back's against the wall. How I'ma tell that man I ain't gonna post his bail after all he did for me while I was locked up?"

"The same way I'm telling you no."

Gage sat down on the bed next to Arrissa and grabbed her gently by her hand. "I understand how you feel but—"

"If you understood how I felt, you wouldn't ask me to do some-thing so stupid."

"Will you listen to me for a minute? I can't start acting funny now, not with all this stuff going on. We have to pull back slowly."

"You just don't get it do you?"

"Naw, I get it. You the one that don't get it. You want to move off emotions all the time, and I can't move like that. You have to trust that I ain't gonna steer you wrong. You with me or not?"

Arrissa sighed. "I'm with you, but if this isn't over soon me and Hakim gonna go and stay with my grandmother until you decide we're more important than your friends."

Gage kissed Arrissa on her forehead. "Thanks babe. And just so you know, you and Hakim are the most important people in my life.

"You said we were only bailing him out, not picking him up too," Arrissa said from the driver's seat of her Infinity. She and Gage were parked out front of the Wilmington Police Station wait-ing for Esco to be released.

"Will you relax," Gage said. "I thought you said you was with me on this, but you been complaining since we got in the car."

"And I'm gonna continue to complain if you keep putting your-self, better yet us, in the middle of this foolishness."

Gage wished his wife would shut up. He just wanted to pick Esco up and take him wherever he needed to be dropped off. Her complaining wasn't going to change anything, except maybe his mood. She was working his last nerve.

"There he go right there, "Gage said, reaching over to the steer-ing wheel and beeping the horn to get Esco's attention. "We gonna drop him off then put this shit behind us. You cool with that?"

Arrissa rolled her eyes then shifted in her seat and stared out the window.

The back door swung open and Esco slid into the backseat. "Good looking out, dawg," Esco said, slapping hands with Gage. "Thanks, Arrissa."

Arrissa pulled out into traffic without saying a word.

"Don't mind her," Gage said. "So what did you get knocked for?"

"I don't know where to begin. My girl got shot yesterday, I ain't even sure if she made it."

Gage and Arrissa looked over at each other at the same time. There was a trace of a smirk on Arrissa's face. The sight of it almost made Gage question his Judas like decision.

"Y'all ain't see that shit on the news?" Esco asked. "I know it made headlines cause' a cop got killed. That's the only reason I got locked up. They said I assaulted an officer at the scene just so they could take me in for questioning."

"I ain't even been watching TV," Gage said.

"Where are we dropping you off?" Arrissa blurted out.

"My car's up there by Monkey Hill. Y'all can drop me off there."

The rest of the short ride was silent. Gage started to check Arrissa for her rudeness right then but decided to wait until they dropped Esco off. There was no telling what might fly out of her mouth if they got into an argument in front of Esco.

When Arrissa pulled up behind Esco's car, Gage noticed a few white men wearing windbreakers bearing CSI on the back of them about twenty yards away taking pictures and collecting what he assumed was evidence. Yellow police tape and orange cones blocked off the side of the street the CSI agents were working. Gage was willing to bet the Wilmington Police Department was working around the clock to find out who killed their comrade.

"I'ma shoot to the hospital," Esco said. "You mind riding up there with me? I don't know what to expect when I get there."

"I got you," Gage said. "Let me holla at my wife for a minute then I'ma hop in the car with you."

"Alright." Esco got out of the car and shut the door.

"I can't fucking believe you," Arrissa yelled. "You just don't get enough. All this stuff going on, and you still want to be in the middle of it."

"First off," Gage said, staring deep into Arrissa's eyes. "Remember who you talking to. I already told you how I feel about things, and I ain't gonna keep repeating myself. You either gonna ride with me or you ain't."

Arrissa looked as if she was about to say something, but Gage put his pointer finger to her lips. "Don't even say nothing. I'll be home in a couple of hours."

Gage reached over the center console and tried to kiss Arrissa on her lips, but she turned her head and gave him her cheek.

"Get out."

"Don't act like that."

"Just get out, Gage."

"As Salaamu alaykum," Gage said opening the passenger door. He knew there was no use fighting.

"Wa alaykum Salaam."

Gage got out of the car and shut the door behind him. He wanted to say more to his wife, let her know everything was going to work out, but she didn't give him a chance. She peeled off without a wave or a beep of the horn. He watched as his wife's car sped down the street wondering if he made the right decision.

As Dirty As It Gets

chapter Twenty seven

Esco's voice broke through the silence in the car, snapping Gage from his thoughts. "You ever just want to pick up and get away?"

Gage turned his attention from the fast moving scenery outside his passenger window and looked over at Esco. "Why you ask that?"

"Cause' that's how I feel. After I'm done with Flip, I'm out. I ain't packing shit but Sinnamon, Shaquan and my money. Fuck the rest of this shit."

"You make it sound a lot easier than it really is."

"How you figure that?"

"Cause' the shit ain't easy. Sometimes things pop up, and you can't walk away when you want."

Esco got off the highway at the exit that led to the hospital. "I hear you, but you wanna know the truth?"

"I just told you the truth. The shit is hard."

"Cause' you make it hard, Gage. Deep down in ya heart you wanna be a part of this shit. You ain't ready to leave the streets alone yet. Any excuse you can come up with to hang on to this shit you gonna use."

"Nah, Es," Gage said, raising his voice. "You got me fucked up. I'm tired of living like this. To be honest, the only reason I ain't living in peace now is cause' I'm stuck in the middle of all this shit you got going on."

"My situation ain't got nothing to do with you."

"It got everything to do with me. Mills is dead and I fucks with

109

you hard, I ain't just gonna play the sideline while my niggas is at war. At the end of the day I am and always will be a real nigga."

The rest of the ride to the hospital was silent. When Esco pulled into the hospital's parking lot he parked then looked over at Gage, his eyes soft but stern, the look of a father trying to guide his son to the right path.

"If you didn't have a family or the desire to change, what you said would make a lot of sense." Esco's voice was smooth and even. "But the realest shit a man in your shoes could ever do, would be to fall back and put his family first. Family is everything. A man that can't see or understand that will never be as real as he think he is."

Gage felt foolish for his childish claim to realness and said nothing as Esco exited the car. He suffocated under the weight of Esco's words for a couple of minutes before he opened the car door and sucked in the cool spring air. His thoughts made his walk to the hospital's entrance long and tiresome.

In the hospital's lobby Gage, spotted Esco at an information desk speaking to a familiar looking Hispanic woman. A smirk crept across his face when he realized just how familiar the woman really was. He wouldn't be the only one feeling foolish this afternoon. He strode to the information desk with his head held high, the taste of revenge dancing on his tongue.

The woman handed Esco a piece of paper that he seemed to study before he stuck it in his back pocket. Esco walked in the direction of the elevator, and Gage approached the desk. The woman's attention was on the computer screen that sat in front of her, but she must've felt his presence. She put one manicured finger in the air and told Gage she'd be with him in a second.

"Can I help you— Anthony?" The woman looked confused
Gage's smirk became a smile. "How have you been Erica?"

"I thought you were in jail."

"I was, but the truth came out. Like I told you then, I was innocent. Come to find out, my ex set me up. She admitted it and my appeal was granted."

"That's great." The sparkle in Erica's eyes could've lit up the darkest corner in the world. "We have a lot of catching up to do.

As Dirty As It Gets

You know I still have the ring you bought me. When can we do lunch?"

"Never."

"Anthony, let me explain." Her words were rushed.

"You could never explain what you did. We was supposed to get married, but you abandoned me when I needed you the most."

A cloud seemed to hover over Erica's head. Her eyes watered, then tears extinguished the spark of love that was in her eyes. Ashes of defeat settled in her pupils, a sight that surprisingly did nothing for Gage. He thought her pain would ease his. But seeing her, as beautiful as the day they met, actually reawakened the beast known as heartbreak.

"I'm sorry." Erica's words were barley a whisper.

"I am too."

There was nothing left to say. Gage walked off, his heart heavier than it should've been. He caught up to Esco at the bank of elevators just as one of the elevator's doors slid open.

They both stepped inside.

Silence.

Esco pressed the button for the fourth floor and the elevator began its ascent.

"Everything cool?" Gage asked.

"She's in ICU, but she's still breathing. I won't really know what's up till I speak to a doctor. I need to see if the baby is alright."

"Insha Allah, everything is cool." There was an awkward pause. "Thanks for what you said in the car. I needed to hear that."

"I would expect you to do the same for me."

The elevator's bell rang, then the doors slid open. Both men stepped out.

Gage followed Esco to a room that was guarded by an overweight police officer that slept in an armless plastic chair with his chin to his chest, his stomach protruding like a pregnant woman's.

"Look at this dude," Esco said as he and Gage walked past the cop and into the hospital room.

Not really wanting to see Sinnamon, Gage leaned against the wall at the entrance of the room. He saw that a woman was seated

111

in a recliner next to Sinnamon's bed, watching TV. Esco stood next to her.

"How is she?" Esco asked.

The woman looked up at Esco. She frowned. "You finally decided to show up I see."

"The only reason I ain't been here is because I got locked up. They just let me out. I came straight here."

"That day I saw you in Riverside. You promised me my daughter was in good hands."

"She is."

"Not laid up in that hospital bed she ain't."

"That wasn't my fault."

"The hell it wasn't."

Gage wanted to yell that everything was Sinnamon's fault. Blood was on her hands. Innocent blood. His wife could've been the one in that hospital bed hooked to machines. And it would've all been Sinnamon's fault.

"How's the baby?" Esco asked.

"Good. Where's my son?"

"With my mom."

"I want to see him."

Esco turned around and faced Gage. "Let me holler at her real quick."

"Do ya thing," Gage said. "It seems like everything is cool, so I'ma call my wife and have her pick me up."

"You sure? I can take you home."

"Naw, I'm good, handle your business."

Esco walked over to Gage. They shook hands then brought each other in for a brotherly hug.

"Good looking out," Esco said, breaking the embrace.

"That ain't about nothing. Holler at me when you get things settled."

"I got you."

"Are you done playing super friend?" Arrissa said the moment Gage got into the car.

"Not right now."

"Yes, now. I need to know so I can have my bags packed the

next time some niggas kidnap me from my house."

"Why you gotta take it there."

"Cause' you can't walk away from your friends." Arrissa pulled away from the hospital.

"I am walking away, but at my pace. Just give me a minute."

"Well, until that minute is up, me and Hakim will be staying with my grandmother."

"You're not moving."

"Me and Hakim are not staying in that house, *you* turned into a death trap, the other night."

"I said, you ain't going anywhere."

"Gage, I already made the arrangements. When you're ready to move out of that house, this state, away from ya fake ass friends, and finally put your family first, we'll come back. Until then, I'ma step up and do what's right for this family.

chapter Twenty eight

It took a few minutes for Sinnamon's eyes to adjust to the bright lights. She looked around and realized she was cuffed to a hospital bed. Alone. Esco immediately flooded her thoughts. She needed to know where he was. The last thing she remembered, he was on his way to her right before the crash. She looked around the room for any signs of him. The only thing she saw that indicated another person was in the room was a tan leather purse that hung on the back of the recliner next to her bed.

A toilet flushed. Sinnamon made an attempt to sit up but it hurt too much to move. She focused her eyes on the door that she figured led to the bathroom, almost expecting Essence to walk out. That was the only female she could think of that would be at her bedside.

When the bathroom's door swung open, Sinnamon couldn't believe her eyes. Her mother was standing in the doorway drying her hands with a paper towel. She looked good too. The skinny, bad skin, sunken face woman she remembered looked to have gained at least thirty pounds. Sinnamon wrestled with the smile that tried to creep across her face. There was no way she'd let Betty know she was even a little bit pleased to see her.

"What are you doing here?" Sinnamon asked.

"I came to make sure you were okay," Betty replied, walking over to Sinnamon's bed. "I've been here every day since I found out what happened. You've been sleep for six days."

"Where's Esco and Shaquan?"

"Esco took Shaquan to his mother's house about an hour ago.

114

He should be back soon. He's been up here a lot. That boy really loves you."

"Too bad you don't."

Betty cast her gaze towards the floor and wiped the palms of her hands against her thighs. She looked up at Sinnamon again, her eyes full of sorrow.

"What's the matter?" Sinnamon asked. "Cat got your tongue?"

"Now is not the time for this, Sinnamon. You need your rest."

"No, this is the perfect time. For all I know I may fall back to sleep, wake up and won't see you again for another few years."

"Sinnamon," Betty's tone was as gentle as a cool summer breeze. "I'm sorry, okay. I know I wasn't the best mother and I'm sorry for that."

"You're a sorry excuse for a mother, that's what you are. Why are you even here?"

Betty wiped the tears that fell from her eyes then took a deep breath. "Baby, I know you're mad, but I can only apologize. I can't change the past. If you don't open up to me with a forgiving heart, my apologies won't mean nothing."

"Your apologies will never mean anything to me." Sinnamon did what she could to hold back her tears, but one escaped and slid down the side of her face. She didn't bother to wipe it. She didn't even know why she was crying in the first place. Betty needed to leave.

"God willing, you'll be a mother soon, Sinnamon. You may make mistakes like me."

"I'm not like you."

"I'm not saying that you are, baby. All I'm saying is that you'd want your child to love you despite the mistakes you may make as a parent. I'm asking you to do the same for me. No matter how angry you are with me I'ma always be your mother and will love you no matter what."

"So is that why you're here? You think you can sweet talk me and simply walk back into my life?"

"No, Sinnamon. I'm here because I love you." Betty removed her purse from the chair and hung it over her shoulder. "And I'ma continue to be here for you. I'ma leave now so you can get some rest, but I'll be back tomorrow as soon as I get off of work. I love you Sinnamon, and I will see you tomorrow."

Sinnamon watched as her mother walked out of the hospital room and couldn't help but wonder if she was really going to come back. Even though she'd never admit it, a part of her hoped she did. Sinnamon closed her eyes, and tried to shake the longing she had for her mother.

"How you feeling?" Esco said.

Sinnamon opened her eyes and saw him walking towards her. He sat the soda and the Burger King bag he was carrying on the night stand that was next to Sinnamon's bed then sat beside her on the bed and kissed her gently on her lips.

"Better, now that you're here," Sinnamon said. "I was worried when I woke up and didn't see you."

"You know I wouldn't leave you up in a hospital by yourself. Me and your mom been here every day."

Sinnamon couldn't understand why Esco would think that she wanted to see her mother. He knew what Betty put her through and should have the same ill feelings towards Betty as she did.

"Why did you let her come see me?" she asked.

"That's your mom. What I'm supposed to tell her, to leave?"
"Yes, you should've told her to leave. You know how I feelabout her. She's a junkie."

"Like you can talk."

Sinnamon's feelings were crushed. She knew what Esco was implying, but she wasn't a junkie. She was nothing like her mother; she would never put drugs before her kids. Not like Betty did.

"How could you say that to me?" Sinnamon's voice was low. "You don't even understand all she put me through. I didn't even have a childhood because of her."

"That don't make it right for you to disrespect her the way you did. I heard the way you was talking to her. That's fucked up. I've been around junkies all my life. You should be thankful she managed to get clean. You could've lost her to the needle."

"That would've been fine by me."

"You don't mean that."

As Dirty As It Gets

Sinnamon rolled her eyes. "Yes, I do."

Esco grabbed her by her hand. "It's alright to be mad, but you can't throw stones when you live in a glass house. And you know what I'm talking about. Now I ain't trying to come down on you cause' we're past that. But you need to be more understanding towards your mom. If I didn't catch you, you could've ended up just like her."

"I'm not her!"

"I ain't say you was."

"Then what are you saying, Ira?"

"I'm saying you need to get off your high horse, and apologize to your mom. Talk to her. She might help you with your problem."

"I don't have a problem." Sinnamon turned her head from Esco. Her gaze landed on the silver handcuffs that were on her wrist.

"Whether you feel you have a problem or not, you need to apologize to your mom."

"I'll think about it."

"Well, you better think soon cause' she's going to be around." Sinnamon glared at Esco. "What do you mean by that?" "She's going to be staying with us for a while."

"No the fuck she isn't."

"She is, and you're going to accept it. I still have to clean up that mess you made. So I'ma be in and out. You gonna need help around the house, especially with Shaquan."

"I don't want her help."

"You have no choice."

chapter
Twenty nine

Bone sat on the couch in one of Flip's townhouses looking at Flip with disgust. Once again Flip was reclined in his La-Z Boy recliner with a nickel-plated .45 automatic on his lap and a lit blunt of PCP between his lips.

"You need to stop smoking that shit so you can focus and tell me about the plan you got," Bone said. "The shit got you looking like you dying anyway."

Flip blew a cloud of smoke in Bone's direction. "I don't give a fuck how I look."

"Well you need to think about your brain then cause' you can't even think when you smoke that shit."

"Listen, don't worry about me." Flip took a deep drag from his blunt, "I'm the fucking boss so worry about what the fuck I tell you to worry about." Smoke wafted out of his mouth with each spoken syllable.

Bone caressed the long barreled .38 revolver he had placed on his lap in case Flip got crazy. He hated being talked down to. At times he thought of killing Flip himself. At the rate Flip was getting high, he and Newz would be better off without him anyway.

"You looking over here like you wanna try me or something," Flip said.

Bone wasn't in the mood for arguing. "Ain't nobody got time for your bullshit, Flip. Just tell me what the fuck is up with this plan you got."

Flip took another pull from his blunt then sat it in the ashtray on the small table that sat next to him. He stared at Bone with eyes that seemed to drift to another land. His expression was on the brink of confusion. He gripped the handle to his gun then pointed it at Bone. "Who the fuck you talking to?" There was an eerie calm in Flip's voice.

Bone snatched his .38 off of his lap and aimed it at Flip's head. If Flip was to so much as flinch he was going to blow his brains all over the living room.

"Ain't nobody scared of you." Bone gripped the handle of his gun tighter and caressed the trigger with his index finger.

A smile slowly crawled across Flip's face.

"See, this is why I fucking love you, dawg," Flip said, placing his gun back on his lap. "You don't back down from nobody. Out of all the young boys I had on my squad you and Newz been the thoroughest."

Bone kept his gun trained on Flip. He wasn't trying to pass a thorough test. He didn't have to. There was no question of what type of person he was.

"Don't ever point a fucking gun at me again, Flip." Bone lowered his gun but maintained his grip on its handle. He placed the gun back on his lap, conveniently pointing it's barrel at Flip as a precaution.

"Where Newz at?" Flip asked.

"I think he went over some bitch crib. He'll probably be back tonight. But fuck that, what's up with the plan you was talking about?"

"I'm ready to head back down Delaware."

"I figured that much. What are you trying to do down there?"

"We moving to Wilmington."

This nigga done lost his mind. "I ain't moving to no Wilmington."

Flip fished his blunt out of the ashtray and relit it. "I already grabbed a three bedroom crib down there on the Westside."

"That shit got you bugging. You trying to make us easy targets. And what about that cop that got killed? I ain't fucking with it."

"If you scared, say you scared."

"If you dumb, say you dumb."

Flip took a drag from his blunt. "My man Newz gonna be with it."

"Not if he got sense."

"Listen, it's a method to my madness, Bone. Just trust me. We move down there, get a little money in the process, and handle them niggas. Two birds, one stone."

"I ain't feeling this shit. We gonna fuck around and get killed down there."

"I know moving down there sounds crazy, but I ain't bugging. I've been handling beef since you been shit'n in pampers. We go down there, blend in and fall back till the time's right. We live with the enemy, dress like the enemy, act like the enemy until—" Flip made an imaginary gun with his hand then pulled the trigger. "Boom. We kill them all."

chapter

Thirty

"I want to hire a nurse," Sinnamon said, sitting at the foot of her hospital bed. She watched Esco stuff the last of her belongings into a large duffle bag. A week had went by since she woke up, and already she was cleared to go home.

Esco zipped the duffle shut, then looked at her with an agitated expression on his face. "That's a waste of money. I ain't doing it."

"I don't need your money. I'll pay for it myself." Sinnamon folded her arms across her chest like a defiant child.

"We ain't even having this discussion." Esco put the duffel bag's strap over his shoulder. "You want to walk, or do you want me to push you in a wheelchair?"

"I want you to hire me a nurse, Ira. That's what I want. It wasn't enough I had to deal with that bitch all week? You're really going to let her live in *my* house?"

Esco's nose flared and his eyebrows knotted together.

"Yeah she gonna live in *our* house. Ya mom did a lot for your ungrateful ass this week. I can't believe you still disrespecting her like that."

"And I can't believe you're still defending her. I'm your wife."

"You sure, cause' my wife would never disrespect her mom the way you do."

A hospital orderly wearing light blue scrubs walked into the room smiling from ear to ear. Sinnamon wondered how he was so happy in a world where death was dominant and mothers refused to be mothers.

"Does she need a wheelchair?" the orderly asked. "I can push her out to your car if you want me to."

"What am I invisible or something? Why are you asking him what to do with me?"

The orderly looked embarrassed. "I figured—"

"You ain't got to explain yourself to her," Esco said. "Go ahead and grab a wheelchair."

"I don't want a damn wheelchair!" Sinnamon carefully lifted herself from the bed. Her legs were weak and almost buckled underneath her. "I want you to hire me a nurse."

Esco glared at Sinnamon then at the orderly.

"Ain't it your job to transport patients?"

"Yeah but—"

"Well, go get the wheelchair then."

The orderly rushed out of the room.

Esco turned back to Sinnamon. "You ain't getting a damn nurse, now sit ya ass down until dude comes back."

The look in Esco's eyes told Sinnamon she may have gotten a little more under his skin than she wanted to. She sat back down on the bed and said nothing. Why couldn't Esco just sympathize with her? She'd been shot, hospitalized, and now her no good mother was trying to weasel her way back into her life. She was sure her mother had some type of motive for showing up unexpected, and more than likely it had something to do with money.

Esco walked over to the large window and stared out of it.

An older female orderly pushed a wheelchair into the room. The look on her face said she was not to be played with. She parked the wheelchair in the middle of the room, then left without saying a word.

Esco didn't even look at Sinnamon when he walked to the wheelchair and pushed it over to her. She sat in the wheelchair without protest. She didn't even complain about the discomfort she felt in her stomach. And Esco didn't say a word as he pushed her out of the room.

Sinnamon stared out the passenger's window as Esco drove 95 south headed to Wilmington. Her thoughts consumed her. She knew she was wrong for acting like a bitch in her hospital room and began to question if she was being too hard on Betty. She had to admit her mother was trying. The crazy thing about it was her mother's efforts seemed sincere. Still, she wasn't ready to let go of the past. She couldn't. It was Betty's fault that her life was upside down and miserable, and she hated her for that.

Sinnamon looked over at Esco and stared at him. He still looked pissed. She was sure he was mad at her for the way she'd been acting but wondered if that was the only thing bothering him. He seemed to have a lot on his mind lately. Maybe the mess she made was taking a toll on him. She felt awful for everything and wished she could help. She wanted to help but she had to think about the baby.

"What are you thinking about?" Sinnamon asked.

Esco looked her way, an annoyed expression on his face. He turned his attention back on the road. "Trust me, you don't want to know."

"Why do you have to be so mean?"

Esco ignored her.

"Talk to me, please. Tell me what's on your mind."

"You really want to know?" Esco asked without taking his eyes off the road.

"Yes."

"I'm over here trying to figure out if I'ma marry your ass or not."

Sinnaman felt her heart shatter. "What do you mean?"

"I ain't sure I can marry a woman that don't respect her mom. I'm saying, if you can't respect your own mom how you going to treat mine?"

"I'd never disrespect your mother, Ira. You know that. The situation with my mother is just—" Sinnamon searched for the right words to express how she felt.

"Is just what?"

"I don't know. It's hard to explain. You'd have to be me to understand how I feel. Please don't judge me for how I act towards her."

"How you treat your mom is a big thing to me. I love my mom more than life itself. It'd be an ugly look if you ever get out of line with her."

Sinnamon sucked her teeth then folded her arms across her

chest. "You don't have to threaten me. I told you I'd never disrespect your mother."

"Prove it to me."

"How?"

"Take it easy on your mom. See what she has to offer. No matter how much you don't like it, she's going to be living with us till you one-hundred percent. Respect her."

Sinnamon sighed. She didn't know if respecting her mother was even possible.

"Alright, Ira, damn. I'll try my best. Don't expect too much though."

Esco looked over at Sinnamon with a silly grin on his face. "You so sexy when you mad."

She tried not to smile but couldn't help it. Esco could make her smile on her worst day. "Whatever boy."

"You are. I can't wait till I can get a taste of that thing," Esco said licking his lips.

Sinnamon's panties dampened. The doctor's orders for her not to have sex for another two weeks flew out the window and scattered across the highway. She was getting some and soon.

She couldn't control the smile on her face when Esco pulled in front of their house. She was so excited to be home she could've pissed herself. She missed everything about her house: her soft carpeted floors, her bed, her pillows comforter, and its homely aroma; the sweet scent like heaven compared to the stale smell of the hospital. Soon as Esco put the car in park she popped the passenger's door open.

"I don't need the wheelchair," Sinnamon said, swinging her legs out the car. She used the top of the door and the edge of the car's roof to pull herself to her feet. A bearable pain shot through her abdomen but she managed to stand up straight and walk.

"Slow down girl," Esco said taking a hold of her arm.

She pushed him away. "I'm okay."

"You sure?"

Sinnamon nodded then took slow and steady steps to the house. The pain in her abdomen dulled but her wounded leg hurt more with each step.

As Dirty As It Gets

Esco went ahead of Sinnamon and opened the front door. She limped into the house and took a deep breath. She wasn't disappointed. Her Glades plug-ins still pumped their lavender scent into the air.

"I have to get out of these clothes." Sinnamon kicked off her sneakers. She'd been dying to do that since she put them on. They weren't uncomfortable, she just didn't like them on her feet. Regardless of what the doctor said she was in the need of a pair of heels. There wasn't a thing wrong with her feet so that was another rule that was going to be broken.

Sinnamon was about to take off her sweatpants but thought about her brother. "Where's Shaquan?" "Your mom figured you'd want a little time to yourself so they staying at her spot tonight. They'll be back tomorrow."

Sinnamon literally bit her tongue. Her mother had no business around Shaquan. She shook her thoughts, then wiggled out of her sweats. She could feel Esco's eyes on her. When she looked back at him she saw him staring at her, lust heavy in his eyes.

"I can't wait to take a shower." She pulled off her shirt.

"I see," Esco said, still staring lustfully.

Sinnamon let Esco help her go up the steps and to the bathroom. He tried to go in the bathroom with her, but she stopped him at the bathroom's door.

"Damn, I can't watch?"

"No, boy." Sinnamon shut the door gently in his face. There was no way she was going to let him see the wild bush that had grown between her thighs. Essence told her when they first met that real women kept themselves well groomed, and a man, hus- band included, should never have to see her not properly groomed.

Sinnamon spent more than two hours in the bathroom. She shaved her pubic area completely bald, then shaved her legs. She showered and washed her hair, leaving it wet and curly. She even clipped, filed and polished her fingernails and toenails. After oiling herself with Vaseline and a pear scent lotion, she looked, smelled and felt like her normal self.

She walked out of the bathroom and into her bedroom as naked as Eve. Esco was laying comfortably in their bed wearing a pair of sweatpants and a wife beater. He looked good enough to eat. Sinnamon walked slowly to the bed, doing her best not to show signs of pain. She climbed onto the bed then crawled on top of Esco and kissed him.

He broke their kiss. "The doctor said—"

Sinnamon put her pointer finger to his lips then kissed him from his neck down to the top of his chest. He sat up and peeled his wife beater off, tossing it to the side. She continued to plant kisses down his body until she reached the elastic of his sweatpants. She pushed his upper body back down on the bed and pulled at his sweats until his manhood was free. She took it in her mouth and sucked it slowly.

Esco let out a slow moan and grabbed a fistful of her hair. "Damn I missed you."

Sinnamon picked up her pace, loving how Esco reacted to her skills. She wanted to please him, show him that she was more than worthy of marrying. She wanted him to see that he needed her as much as she needed him.

"Damn—Slow—Hold—Hold on a minute baby."

Sinnamon stopped and looked up at Esco confused. She thought she was doing a good job. Why would he want her to stop?

"Come here," Esco said.

Sinnamon crawled on top of Esco. He flipped her onto her back then peered into her eyes. Her pussy became so wet it felt like a river was between her legs. He kissed her neck tenderly then dragged his tongue to her breast. His tongue danced around each of her nipples. She couldn't remember the last time she felt so good.

He trailed his tongue further down her body, stopping at the wound on her abdomen. He kissed the pain away then continued his trip down and found her clitoris. Sinnamon's body exploded with pleasure. She screamed out Esco's name and grabbed at his shoulders and head. Her grip settled on one of the pillows that were on the bed. She put the pillow over her face and bit down as another wave of pleasure took hold of her body and dragged her into an ocean of orgasms.

Her legs trembled and her body felt weak but she still wanted more. She tossed the pillow then pulled Esco up from between her thighs.

"I want you inside me," she whispered.

Esco eased himself inside of her. His strokes were slow and gentle. Her body knew of no pain, only pleasure. Everything about the sex was perfect. The closeness of their bodies, the tender way Esco touched her, the way they came at the same time; it was all perfect and she fell in love all over again.

Sinnamon cuddled next to Esco, laying her head on his chest. "When are we getting married?"

"Soon, baby. Real soon. I just need to handle that bullshit first." Sinnamon looked up into Esco's eyes. "I don't want to wait. We're not promised tomorrow, look at Essence. She's gone. And look what happened to me. I could've died, and if I have to die, I want to at least die as your wife."

Esco smiled then kissed her on her forehead. "Make arrangements. We'll get married as soon as you get things together."

chapter
Thirty one

Rapper Meek Mill's Flamers Two CD blared throughout the smoky interior of Flip's Lincoln Continental. He was at a red light finishing his third blunt of PCP. He let his window down then took one last deep drag from the blunt, letting it burn down to his fingertips, and flicked it out the window. Despite being high enough to kiss the moon, he fished another PCP filled blunt from his ashtray and lit it. The light turned green.

Flip slammed his foot on the gas pedal. The Lincoln took off like an all-black missile through the Westside of Wilmington. He scanned his surroundings, hoping to see a female he could take back to his place but was disgusted with what he saw. The only women stalking the area looked to be junkies; which made sense being that it was closing in on 1:30 a.m. on a cold Wednesday morning. He should've stayed in the house with Newz and the young girls that Newz met earlier that day. They looked good, and the one that was supposed to be for him was actually over twenty-one. The only problem, she looked so much like Monica it was scary.

Monica…He still couldn't believe she was gone. There wasn't a doubt in his mind that Esco and that bitch Sinnamon had something to do with her murder. He hated every minute the two of them breathed. They should've been dead. He'd been living in Wilmington for two weeks and hadn't made a move yet. But that was about to change. He looked over at his passenger seat, an all-black Tec-9; somebody was going to die tonight.

He pressed his foot harder on the gas pedal and barreled towards the north side. The possibility that Esco would be on the block so late was slim but he was sure somebody would be out there. It didn't matter who. As long as when the smoke cleared, somebody was laid out on the concrete dead.

It only took Flip five minutes to reach Concord Ave. Just as he figured, a few people were posted up in front of the barbershop. He made a left at Concord Ave. and Jefferson and rode Jefferson down two blocks before he parked. He stubbed his blunt out, then jumped out of the Lincoln, leaving it running, and walked casually up the block bearing the Tec in his hand like it was legal.

Flip walked down the block on the opposite side of the street the barbershop was on. His eyes were on four men and a woman. They were so busy running their mouths they didn't pay him any attention. When he got closer, he realized two of them were shooters from the night he was almost killed at Night on Broad. He'd never forget a face, especially the faces of men that tried to murder him.

One of his attempted killers was on crutches. He couldn't believe the nigga was dumb enough to be on the block in the middle of a serious beef in that condition. He must've wanted to die. And that was cool with Him.

This was Flip's first time seeing the other dudes. One was young, maybe eighteen, and the other was with a woman. It was evident from the dishevelment of the man and woman's clothing they were junkies, innocent from all the bullshit that had taken place, but that didn't matter.

Flip aimed the Tec and fired as he walked closer to the small crowd. He fired slow then rapid then slow again trying to prevent the gun from jamming.

Feathers flew out of the jacket of the man on the crutches. He dropped to the ground first, followed by the other shooter, then the young boy.

The woman sprinted away fast enough to beat Flo-Jo in a 100-meter dash and escaped the bullets. Her friend wasn't so lucky. The idiot dropped whatever drugs he copped and tried to pick them up before running. He caught at least one bullet in his ass.

Flip loved every minute of the chaos.

WASIIM

"I'ma kill all you pussies!" He yelled over the gunfire.

He continued to shoot until every bullet in the gun was gone. He back peddled up the block then turned around and ran back to his car grinning.

"I hope they all die," he said once he was behind the wheel of the Lincoln. He relit his blunt and inhaled deeply before pulling off. "I hope all of them mutha-fuckas die."

chapter Thirty Two

"Babe," Arrissa said with excitement in her voice, "I was looking on the Internet and found some nice houses in Florida."

"That's what's up." Gage tried to match his wife's enthusiasm but knew he failed the moment the words crossed his lips.

She glared at him then rolled her eyes.

"What's all that for?" Gage asked.

Arrissa sucked her teeth. "You just don't care do you?"

Gage let out a long breath. He was getting tired of talking about moving. That's all Arrissa talked about when they were together. *When are we going to move? Where are we going to move?* He had a place for her to move alright, back home where her ass belonged. It didn't make any sense, as grown as he was, to have to meet up with his wife in her grandmother's dining room.

"We already talked about this," Gage said. "We gonna move when the time's right."

"And when is that?"

"I told you when things cool down."

"You need to come up with a better answer because I'm tired of that one."

"Come here for a minute."

Arrissa gave him a look that said she wasn't going to budge.

"You gonna act like that? I came all the way in town to spend some quality time with my loving wife, and you gonna act like you don't love me. All I want is a hug."

Arrissa sucked her teeth again. "You make me sick," she said, getting out of her seat. She walked around the table and stood next to him.

WASIIM

He pulled her down onto his lap then kissed her on her neck. "That wasn't so hard was it?"

"No, it wasn't. Just like you giving me a better answer to when are we going to move isn't that hard."

Gage kissed her on her neck again, this time nibbling on it a little bit.

"Boy, if you don't cut it out. You know my nana is upstairs. Hakim too."

"Let's go in to the bathroom real quick." Gage groped all over his wife's body. His dick, harder than a piece of steel, and felt as if it was going to rip through his jeans. He wanted his wife bad. They hadn't had sex since she moved out, and that few weeks felt more like a few years.

Arrissa moaned. "Why you gotta be so nasty."

"Cause' you love me that way," Gage said, sliding his hands up Arrissa's tee shirt. He cupped both of her breast and caressed them the way he knew she liked it. Massaging them and her erect nipples at the same time.

"Come on babe, let's go in the bathroom. I promise I'll be quick."

Arrissa looked into his eyes. A devilish smile eased across her face. "You're serious aren't you?"

"Why wouldn't I be?"

"Alright, but you better make sure you hurry up."

They couldn't make it to the bathroom fast enough. Gage felt like a teenager sneaking off to go have sex for the first time.

"Abu," a little voice called out.

Gage froze in his tracks. He couldn't believe what was happening. Why would Hakim come downstairs when he was so close to victory? He was going to ignore his son and hurry into the bathroom, but that idea was shredded the moment Arrissa stopped and turned around.

"What are you doing up little man?" Arrissa asked in the sweetest voice Gage ever heard.

"I wanted to see my Abu," the little cock blocker said.

Gage looked at his son, and despite his disappointment he grinned. It seemed like Hakim looked more like him every day.

132

As Dirty As It Gets

"How you greet the Muslim when you see him?" Gage asked.

"As salaam lakem," Hakim said, mispronouncing the Islamic greeting.

"It's as salaamu alaykum," Gage corrected.

"I'ma leave you two alone," Arrissa said. "I'll be in the living room. Don't worry, we'll finish what we were talking about later. She winked at Gage then walked out of the dining room.

For the next couple of hours Gage talked to and played with his son. They went over the first chapter of the Qur'an and the movements of the prayer. Gage couldn't believe how fast Hakim caught onto things.

Before Gage realized it, it was after one o'clock in the morning. He needed to send Hakim to bed before Arrissa changed her mind about that quickie.

"Well little Muslim, it's getting late and you need to go to sleep. Good Muslims go to bed early so they can get up for morning salaat."

Gage got up from the dining room table and walked into the living room. Hakim followed closely behind him. They found Arrissa seated on the couch with her legs tucked underneath her. She was reading a real estate magazine, probably looking for another house somewhere he didn't want to move. The sight of the magazine would've soured his mood if he didn't notice she had slipped into a nightgown; an indication they were still on for that quickie.

Hakim ran over to Arrissa and hugged her.

"Good night," he said.

"Good night, sweetie."

Hakim broke their embrace then looked up at his father. "When are we going back home with you, Abu?"

Gage looked at Arrissa for help.

She offered none.

"Insha Allah, soon," Gage said after a few seconds.

"Tomorrow?" Hakim looked at Gage with pleading eyes.

As much as he wanted to tell his son yes, they'd all be going home together tomorrow, he told him the truth. "No, not tomorrow but insha Allah, soon."

Hakim looked as if he was going to say something else but

didn't. He simply ran over to his father and hugged him. Gage scooped Hakim up and wrapped his arms around him. He loved his son more than words could describe.

Gage put Hakim down and watched him sprint noisily up the stairs. He held his breath, praying Hakim didn't wake Arrissa's grandmother up.

"It don't make no sense what you're doing to your son." Arrissa's words were like a jackhammer, loud and disturbing.

Gage flopped down next to her, hoping a new argument wasn't brewing. He caressed her calf and tried to inch his hand up to her thigh.

"Stop!" She swatted his hands away with the magazine. "We need to talk about this."

"Soon as we done in the bathroom." Gage's hands found Arrissa's body again but were swiftly smacked down one by one.

"I said stop," Arrissa said, raising her voice. "We need to talk about how your decisions are affecting your son."

"Stop talking so loud before you wake your grandma up," Gage said in a harsh whisper.

Arrissa threw the magazine at Gage, hitting him in his chest. "I'm not worried about that right now." Her voice grew louder. "And neither should you."

"Damn, Arrissa, what the fuck you want me to say?" Gage still kept his voice low.

"That we're moving."

"I already told you we are. How many times do you want me to say it?"

"I want a date."

"Next month."

"When next month?"

"Thirty days from today. Where?"

"Wherever you want." Gage would've agreed to move to the South Pole if that would've shut his wife up and got her into the bathroom.

A smile beamed across Arrissa's face. "You promise?"

"Yes, Arrissa, I promise."

Arrissa squealed like a little girl. She picked up her magazine, opened it, then shoved the open page in Gage's face. "We're moving here. I'ma call the realtor tomorrow."

Gage grabbed the magazine and looked at the house. It was in a town just outside of Miami that he never heard of before but he had to admit it was nice, very nice; two stories, stone, with a little bit of vinyl on the sides, big front yard and even bigger backyard. Perfect for barbeques and family gatherings, the captions read. Five bedrooms. Six bathrooms; three full, three half. Why the place had so many bathrooms was beyond him.

He skipped the rest of the description and searched for the only two things that really mattered; if it had a basement and the price. The basement was man cave ready, but the price: $750,000. Damn that was a lot of money. But if it would shut her up, then that's what she'd get.

"I'm cool with it." Gage sat the magazine down on the couch. Arrissa leaped into his lap, hugging and kissing him.

"I love you. I love you. I love you."

Gage slid his hands up her nightgown and rubbed her ass. She wasn't wearing any panties. He slipped his middle finger in her juicy slot. "Let's go in the bathroom."

"Come on," she said.

"Arrissa!" The frail, but loud voice caused Gage's hard dick to go limp.

"Yes, Nana," Arrissa yelled back.

"It's almost two o'clock in the morning. Tell your friend good night."

"He's my husband."

"He ain't put no ring on your finger, but if that's what you want to call him, he still needs to go home."

Arrissa's grandmother didn't quite understand Arrissa's Islamic marriage to Gage. She didn't like the fact that they didn't wear wedding rings and didn't even go through the courts to make their marriage legal. A simple contract through a masjid wasn't good enough for her. Gage figured that was the reason she gave him such a hard time.

"He's leaving now, Nana." Arrissa looked at Gage with apologetic eyes.

Gage got up from the couch. "Don't even worry about it."

"I'll make it up to you tomorrow, okay?"

"If you say so." Gage didn't want to wait until the next day. He wanted his now, and since that wasn't going to happen he just wanted to get out of the house before he exploded. He went into the dining room, grabbed his coat, then stormed back into the living room and kissed his wife on her lips. "I'll let myself out."

"I love you."

"Love you too. I'll call you when I get home."

Gage drove away from Arrissa's grandmother's house in complete silence, heated that he was just kicked out. It wasn't humanly possible for him to go through such a humiliating experience again without spazzing out. Arrissa needed to get her priorities together, and if she really wanted that expensive ass house in Florida, he'd better be at the top of her list of things to do.

Forcefully, he peeled the sour thoughts of his wife off of his mind and shifted his thinking to Hakim. He smiled. His son was something special, truly a blessing from Allah. If he didn't do anything else right in life, Gage prayed he'd be a good father. He promised himself years ago, when he was a child, that he'd never be anything like his father. A man he'd rarely seen. A man that didn't teach him how to fight, ride a bike or talk to girls. A man that taught him absolutely nothing. The only good his father did, besides contribute to bringing him in the world, was give him the drive to be better than him.

Gage chuckled, disgusted with himself. How the hell was he going to be any better than his father when he was doing everything to take himself away from his own son? If he didn't wind up back in prison, there was a good chance he'd be killed just like his father. And where would that leave Hakim?"

Flashing lights broke Gage's train of thought. He looked up and realized he was on Washington Street headed towards Concord Avenue. From what he could see, several emergency vehicles were parked on the Avenue. At that time of night, it could only mean one thing...somebody was dead.

Gage swallowed the lump in his throat. He knew he should've turned off of Washington Street and took another street to get to the highway and go home, but he kept straight. He had to see what happened. He drove a few more blocks then parked a half-block from the chaos. Again, something told him to go home. Whatever happened wasn't his business, and there was nothing he could do about it.

Ignoring the voice in his head, Gage got out of his car and walked up Twenty-third and Washington, hoping that whoever was dead was some outsider that didn't belong on the block. It'd be even better if Flip had gotten himself killed trying to make a move.

His moment of hope was short lived. In the mix of the crowd he spotted a neighborhood crack feen that had been around long enough to watch just about all of the local hustlers grow up. Tears were streaming down her face. Somebody from the hood was gone.

"Gator," Gage called out.

The feen turned around. When she spotted Gage she made a beeline straight for him.

"Somebody killed the young boy Vic and shot Clark up real bad," Gator blurted out. "I don't think Clark gonna make it. I was out there. He was bleeding so bad. Out his mouth, nose; blood was everywhere. That nigga was just shooting and shooting. Almost shot me too."

"How many people was shooting?"

"Just one."

"You ever see him before?"

"Naw, I ain't never seen him."

"What he look like?"

Gator closed her eyes for a second then popped them back open. "He was kinda tall, light skinned and had one of those beards like you."

Flip, Gage thought. "Who all was out here when it happened?"

"Me, Bubba, Vic, Clark and Reef."

"Did Reef get hit? Where he at now?"

"Naw, he ain't get shot. He over there across the street sitting on the steps." Gator pointed across the street where Reef was sitting alone with his head down.

"Alright, Gator, I'ma holla at you later. I'ma check on Reef real

137

quick."

Gage walked across the street over to where Reef was seated. He could smell weed smoke before he even made it over to the steps that Reef was on. Smoking with a bunch of cops around was crazy, especially since Reef was on probation.

"What's good?" Gage asked sitting down.

"Ain't nothing good. Clark all hit up and that nigga killed little Vic. That little nigga just turned sixteen yesterday." Reef extended the blunt he was smoking to Gage.

Gage declined it. He wasn't on probation but wasn't interested in getting high. He needed to stay focused.

"That shit is fucked up," Reef said. "What niggas supposed to say to Tiny?"

Gage couldn't answer that. There was nothing you could say to a woman who loses her sixteen-year-old son; her only child. "I don't know, but tell her I'll pay for the funeral when you talk to her."

A glint of resentment flashed in Reef's eyes. "Throwing money around ain't gonna change shit. We need to kill that nigga."

Reef was right, Flip needed to be killed, but there was nothing he could do about it. He was done with the beef. His money was all he could offer. Outside of that he was of no use. He had to think about his son.

"Y'all will get that nigga eventually," Gage said. Reef glared at him. "Fuck you mean y'all?"

Gage could've kicked himself for letting his tongue slip like that. "I ain't mean it like that, so don't take it that way."

"How the fuck I'm supposed to take it?" Reef stood up and looked down on Gage. He took a drag from his blunt then tossed it.

"You've been acting real halfhearted since this shit popped off. Don't be playing both sides." Reef shot Gage a harsh look then walked off without saying another word.

Gage watched Reef walk away, wondering if he'd have to kill him. Reef's eyes screamed he'd kill Gage without a problem if it came to that. To survive, Gage was willing to do whatever it took. Friends sometimes turned to enemies whether you wanted them to or not. Gage understood that well.

chapter Thirty Three

"I'm telling you," Esco said to Reef, "Gage is with us one-hundred percent." The two men sat alone in Off The Ave Barbershop, discussing Reef's run in with Gage after last night's shooting.

"I know you fucks with Gage tough," Reef said, "I do too, but main man heart ain't in this one. You should've heard the nigga talking about, *y'all* gonna get that nigga, like he ain't got nothing to do with this shit."

"If you ask me he ain't got nothing to do with this shit. The nigga just gave all that time back. He got a wife and a son. He need to be somewhere out the way, trying to get his life together."

Reef looked at Esco like he was speaking in tongues. "Once he made the decision to get involved, he committed his self to see this shit through. Ain't no change of heart in war. And if that nigga having a change of heart, we need to be putting together a plan to knock his fucking head off cause ain't no telling how else his heart is changing. Niggas heart might be telling him to change sides."

Reef made a valid point, but Esco had never known Gage to be a shifty dude. Since they'd known each other, Gage showed him nothing but thoroughness and loyalty. The reason Gage was even involved with the whole situation was due to his loyalty to his friends. More than once Gage had made it clear who he was with by putting everything on the line. And being that he had so much to lose that meant a lot.

"I hear what you saying and everything," Esco said, "but I don't think Gage is having a change of heart how you saying he is. The nigga Flip killed his right-hand man, so that alone is enough for him to never fuck with Flip again. If I ever see a clear sign that he's playing the fifty, I'll handle that. Other than that, we ain't even going to discuss this no more."

The door to the barbershop swung open. Detective Johnson stumbled in. He looked terrible. His beard was matted and dry, his eyes red and glassy. The shirt he wore was untucked and wrinkled like he slept in it for weeks. A tie hung loosely from his neck, and he held a battered water bottle in his hand.

The detective staggered over to the barber chair next to Esco and sat in it. He twisted off the cap of the water bottle, and the strong smell of liquor immediately assaulted Esco's nostrils.

"When is it going to stop?" Detective Johnson said. He took a gulp from the water bottle then twisted the cap back on.

Esco looked over at Reef who had a smirk on his face. Esco had to fight to keep himself from smiling too. He was more than amused at the sight of the drunken detective.

"Don't y'all care about human life?" The detective said. "Why do y'all keep killing each other?"

"Man, get the fuck outta here with that bullshit," Reef said. "We ain't kill nobody. That was our friend murdered last night. Not that you give a fuck."

"I give a fuck. Y'all the ones that don't give a fuck. How many friends do you have to lose before you let me help? I know you guys have some sort of beef going on."

"That's where you're wrong," Esco said. "We ain't beefing and we don't know shit about nothing. So you might as well get up and leave. You wasting your time if you think we got some information."

"Bullshit!" The detectives poppy eyes widened with rage. He jumped out of his chair and pointed at Esco. "That's bullshit and you know it. I know you mother fuckers know something."

Esco and Reef both chuckled.

"You mother fuckers think this shit is funny. My partner died because of the bullshit you got going on." Foam caked at the corners of Detective Johnson's mouth, "I'm trying to give you sons of bitches a break here. Keep giving me your ass to kiss, that's fine by me. I'ma be the one to get the last laugh though."

"Well, laugh then," Reef said.

"Come on, fellas. This is off the record. Your little street reps won't be touched. I promise, I won't repeat anything you tell me. I'm just looking for a lead."

Esco didn't feel the slightest bit of sympathy for the detective. If fact, if Esco had it his way, Detective Johnson would be buried right next to his partner.

"Like I said, we don't know shit," Esco said. "So leave."

"Okay," Detective Johnson said. "I'll leave, but remember I tried to cut you a break. The hammer is going to come down, and I'ma make sure y'all feel it." Detective Johnson walked to the door and pushed it halfway open. He looked back at Esco, then to Reef. "May your souls burn in the lowest depths of hell."

Chapter Thirty Four

"I see you're excited about your wedding," Betty said.

Sinnamon looked up from her wedding edition of STYLE Magazine. Her mother comfortably sat on the opposite end of the sofa with her legs tucked underneath her. The woman's voice was as irritating as someone raking their nails across a chalkboard. The cheesy ass grin on her face was just as annoying. Sinnamon couldn't understand for the life of her why Betty was always so damn chipper. Day after day she went above and beyond to be a total bitch, but each day Betty came back unfazed.

"Yes, Mother, I'm soooo excited." Sinnamon rolled her eyes. She almost laughed out loud as she resumed looking through the magazine. Her indignity towards her mother was the new highlight of her now boring, trapped-in-the-house life.

Suddenly, Betty snatched the magazine out of Sinnamon's hands and flung it across the living room.

"Bitch are you craz—" A solid open hand to her cheek caused Sinnamon's head to snap to the right.

"I'm sick of this shit," Betty yelled, standing in front of her, pointing a stiff finger only millimeters away from her face. "I'm just plain sick and tired of it. You are not going to continue to disrespect me, Sinnamon. I don't care if this is your house. I'm your mother, you're going to learn to respect me."

Sinnamon was a blink away from tears. She still couldn't believe Betty smacked her. The left side of her face felt as if it'd been attacked by bees. She placed her hand on her cheek and stared at Betty, not knowing what to do. The woman looked so possessed, Sinnamon was afraid to move.

As Dirty As It Gets

"I wish I could, but I can't change the past Sinnamon." Tears ran from Betty's eyes, extinguishing the lingering anger on her face. "I suffered just as much as you if not more. Do you know what it's like to have to sell your body just to get high? Do you know how many times I've been raped, beaten and abused? I didn't get high because I wanted to. Your father got me hooked on that shit, then my body needed it."

"That didn't make it right for you to leave me." Sinnamon was crying tears of her own now. "I was only ten, and you left me on my own with a child to raise. You left me and Shaquan for dead."

"I didn't want you and your brother to see me the way I was. I did what I felt was the right thing. I knew Ms. Jones would be there for y'all, and I made sure y'all had food stamps. If nothing else I made sure y'all ate good. Don't I get credit for something."

"So what, we ate okay, what about my childhood? Me getting picked on everyday because of the clothes I was forced to wear. Taking care of Shaquan. You don't understand my pain, Mom."

"And you don't understand mine," Betty said lowering her voice. She sat beside Sinnamon and took her hands into hers. "Baby, in life we have to travel the path God chooses for us. Our paths may not have been smooth, but they made us who we are today. We made it through all the bumps and bruises. Look at you." Betty squeezed Sinnamon's hands. "You did a wonderful job with Shaquan. You have a beautiful home, plenty of money, and you're about to marry a handsome young man that loves you. Do you know how many people would trade their hands in for yours?"

"Mom, it's not that simple for me. Things may look sweet on the outside, but I'm hurt—" Sinnamon pointed to her heart. "Here. I'm not proud of how I got some of the things I have, and the way things look some days, I don't even know how long this fairytale will last. I'm sure you know what Ira does, and I couldn't begin to explain some of the things I've done. I don't know my next move or what's in store for me in the future. To be honest—" Sinnamon looked Betty square in the eyes. "I'm just preparing for death."

A look of confusion crossed Betty's face as she repeated Sinnamon's words.

"Only God knows how much longer I have left on this earth,"

Sinnamon said. "All I want to do is get married, live right for at least a little while, and ask God to forgive me for all my sins." Sinnamon wiped her wet face with the backs of her hands. "And just maybe, he'll let me through the gates of Heaven."

Betty pulled Sinnamon to her chest and hugged her tightly. "Honey, God will forgive you if you sincerely repent and live right. Don't you even worry about that. You just continue to pray and do what it is you need to do. Things will work out for the best and know that I'ma always pray for you."

The warmth of her mother's hug and words melted the thick layers of ice that weighed Sinnamon's heart down for so long. She squeezed Betty as tight as she could, sobbing into her bosom. Finally, after all these years, she felt what it was like to experience her mother's love.

Esco walked into the house feeling like he had the weight of the world on his shoulders. Vic's funeral, an event Esco wished he didn't have to attend, was in the morning. It broke his heart to know Vic was gone. He'd watched the young boy grow up. A part of him blamed himself for Vic's death. He could've barred him from the block, maybe even forced him to go to school. Instead, he opted to teach him the ropes, figuring Vic would wonder to another block and get involved in the streets anyway. At least if he was on the Avenue, the block he grew up on, he was safe.

"Damn, what I miss?" Esco asked when he noticed Sinnamon and Betty huddled on the living room floor. A bunch of magazines were sprawled out in front of them, and Sinnamon was actually smiling, something he'd never seen her do when Betty was around. Sinnamon looked up and spotted Esco. Her smile stretched further across her face. She jumped up, clutching some of the magazines in her hand, and ran over to him, almost knocking him down with a hug.

"What do you think about these colors for the wedding?" She asked, holding the magazine in front of Esco's face.

Esco stared at the colors, white and blue. "I'm cool with whatever you choose."

"Come on, baby, you have to get more involved." Sinnamon poked her bottom lip out and gave him the puppy dog look.

As Dirty As It Gets

Esco wasn't in the right frame of mind to discuss wedding details. He didn't even think it was a good time to get married. Too much was going on. "I'll leave it up to you ladies." He faked a smile then headed for the stairs.

"Girl, leave that man alone," Betty said, looking at Esco warily. "You know men don't know nothing anyhow."

Sinnamon let out an exaggerated breath then stomped back over to her mother.

Esco escaped up the stairs and into his bedroom. He flopped down backwards on his bed and sank into his Tempurpedic mattress. He stared at his black, glitter coated ceiling. It felt as if he was staring at the stars. For a moment he was at ease but that quickly faded. Visions of Vic in his casket and Clark lying in the hospital, clinging to his life, incinerated his moment of peace.

Murder. That was the dominant thought on his mind. If he could get a lead on Flip, all the bullshit would be over. The hide and seek game Flip was playing was driving him crazy. Flip attacking Vic's funeral like he did Essence's wouldn't be the most pleasant thing for Vic's family, but Esco prayed the mother fucker showed up. A curse, but most definitely a gift in its own right. Everybody from the avenue would be strapped and ready to kill.

The bedroom door opened. Esco hoped it wasn't Sinnamon coming to sling more wedding magazines in his face

She entered the room, her hands magazine free. Her hair was pulled back into a ponytail just the way he liked it. His soon to be wife was a dime times ten. Each time he laid eyes on her was like the first time.

"How are you feeling?" Sinnamon asked, crawling into bed with him. She settled next to him and rested her head on his chest.

"Fucked up. Vic's funeral is tomorrow, and Clark is still in ICU."

"Is there anything I can do to help?"

"Actually it is." Esco knew Sinnamon wouldn't like what he was about to suggest, but he figured he'd spit it out anyway. "I think you should push the wedding back a couple of months."

Sinnamon sat up shaking her head from side to side. "No, Ira, I'm sorry but we're keeping that date."

WASIIM

"Babe, just hear me out."

"There's nothing to hear."

"I don't think it's safe. What if something happens?"

"You believe in God, right?" Sinnamon peered into Esco's eyes.

"You know I do," Esco said, not knowing where the conversation was about to go.

"Then you know he controls all things. If something bad is going to happen, it's going to happen regardless if we get married or not."

"Seventeen days ain't enough time to get shit together, babe."

"Ira, I understand your concerns, and I know things could be dangerous, but we've waited long enough. Like I told you before, if I die, I want to die your wife."

It was obvious Sinnamon wasn't going to budge. There was no use fighting with her. He either had to crush her feelings and cancel the wedding himself or ride the wave and see what happened.

Sinnamon straddled him. Looking up at her he knew he couldn't spoil her moment. Not right now. Maybe in a few days he'd be able to talk some sense into her.

"Alright, we can keep the damn date."

Sinnamon's face lit up like a kid on Christmas. "I love you baby."

"I love you too," Esco said, wondering how and if he was going to cancel the wedding.

chapter Thirty Five

"Fuck," Detective Johnson yelled. With one swoop of his long arm he knocked everything off his desk. He collapsed on the floor feeling defeated. He'd just gotten back from the Long Shoreman Hall where Vic's family had a dinner following the funeral and didn't get even a small lead. Nothing stood out to him at the funeral. No arguing, no fighting, nothing.

The burial was the same, and at the dinner the family seemed to turn their noses up at him. He tried to speak with a few people but was quickly turned down with sharp words. Some even accused him of not doing his job.

Johnson looked around at the mess he made. His gaze fell on a framed picture of Detective Burton. He picked the picture up and stared at it. "Don't be disappointed, I'm trying."

He sat the picture down, then picked up his gin filled water bottle lying conveniently on its side next to him. He twisted the bottle's cap off and took a gulp. The liquor burned his chest but felt good. If he didn't need anything else, he needed a drink.

Detective Johnson's office door swung open, and his supervisor, Dan, stuck his head in.

"Everything alright in here?" Dan said.

"Yeah, I'm cool, Dan."

Dan walked into the office, shutting the door closed behind him. He strode with his hands in his pockets over to Johnson's empty desk and sat down on it. He stared at Johnson.

"You sure you're okay?" Dan asked. "Cause you look like shit. I don't want to pull you off your case, but I will if I have to."

"I understand what you're saying, but I'm fine. Don't worry

about me. I have everything under control."

"I really insist you take a vacation. You'll be paid for it and it'll give you time to get your head together. You haven't taken a day off since Burton passed."

Take a day off for what. Johnson thought to himself. There was no way he was going to sit at home relaxing while his partner's killer ran the streets freely.

"How about I take you up on that offer after I crack this case?"

Dan stood to his feet. "Suit yourself. I understand you want to bring these scumbags down and, I don't blame you. Just be careful. And stop drinking. That's only going to screw up your judgment."

Johnson watched Dan stroll out of his office. The moment Dan shut the door, Johnson twisted the cap off his water bottle and finished the rest of his gin.

"So what the fuck we gonna do now?" Beefy asked, sitting behind the wheel of his Cadillac.

"Shit, I don't know," Esco said, staring out the passenger window at all the cars in the Long Shoreman's parking lot. He was pissed Flip didn't show up to the funeral. From the looks of things, he wasn't coming to the dinner either. "I was counting on that nigga showing up today."

"That nut ass detective showed up. That's probably why he ain't come."

"I don't even think that's the case. Dude playing a vicious game right now. He's gonna keep popping up trying to off niggas until he gets what he wants."

The car fell silent for a moment.

"You really love that girl don't you?" Beefy asked.

Esco felt there was a hidden message within Beefy's question and struggled not to be offended. Beefy had a right to feel how he felt. Sinnamon was just another bitch to Beefy. In any other case it would've been money over bitches for Esco too, but this time things were different.

Esco looked over at Beefy. "Understand this my nigga. I love Sinnamon more than most niggas will ever understand. She's my heart. But don't get it fucked up. The way shit went down, this whole beef shit ain't about me choosing to ride with my girl. Flip chose to go this route. He killed Essence without even giving me a chance to straighten shit out. I know she don't mean nothing to you, but she was like a little sister to me. At the end of the day it is what it is. I'ma rock all the way out for my peoples. Sinnamon is gonna be my wife soon, and as her husband I'ma see to it that she's protected. If you feel this shit ain't worth fighting for, ain't no love lost. You still my nigga."

Beffy looked offended. "It ain't even like that. You my nigga right or wrong. I'll never turn my back on you. I just never saw you feeling a chick like you feel Sinnamon. That's why I asked."

Esco chuckled at himself for taking such an offensive stance for nothing. He stuck his fist across the armrest and gave Beefy a pound.

"So what's our next move?" Beefy asked.

"We ain't really got no options. I guess we gotta wait it out and try to catch this nigga slipping."

"What about your wedding, it's in a couple of weeks, right? You think he might show up there?"

Esco knew that was definitely a possibility. That's why he wanted to cancel it in the first place. He didn't want to risk the lives of his friends and family.

"I was thinking about pushing that shit back a few months. Sinnamon ain't really trying to hear that, but I'd rather wait till this shit is done and over with."

"I think you should go through with it," Beefy said. "We need that nigga to pop up."

"That shit too risky," Esco said.

"It ain't gotta be."

"How you figure that?"

"It ain't risky if it's a trap to begin with."

Beefy had Esco's attention now. "Trap like how?"

"The same way we was prepared at Vic's and Mills' funerals, we'll be ready at your wedding."

"That shit was different. We couldn't stop no funeral, so we had to do what we had to do. We ain't gotta have the wedding."

"I feel you, but I got a plan that I know will work."

"What's your plan?"

WASIIM

"We can have that shit in the middle of Banning Park. That way if them niggas do show up, the people at the wedding will be a good distance away from where them niggas enter. You know the park big as shit."

Esco nodded in agreement. "If you count everybody from up the way that will ride, it's a lot of us," Beefy said. "Everybody strap up, spread out and protect the wedding. Ain't no way them niggas gonna get close enough to do any real damage. What you think?"

Esco thought for a moment. Beefy's plan was some real movie script shit, but as crazy as it seemed it made sense. It had its flaws though. Mainly the fact that it didn't guarantee the safety of those attending the wedding.

"I can't say I don't think it'll work," Esco said. "But I'm not sure I'm with it. Give me some time to think it over."

chapter
ThIrTY sIX

Gage swerved Arrissa's Infinity into the Getty's gas station on Market Street and pulled up alongside one of the pumps.

"You don't have to treat my car like that," Arrissa said.

Gage turned around to Hakim who sat quietly in the backseat. "You want something from the store?"

"Some candy."

"What kind?"

"A Snickers!"

The smile on his son's face brought Gage some joy but not enough to kill his attitude. Arrissa was working his nerves by staying at her grandmother's house. He'd spent all day with her and Hakim after he left Vic's funeral. Now she wanted to go home. Not home as in the house they shared together, but home to her grandmother, which meant sex was out of the question.

"Can you get me a Pepsi?" Arrissa asked.

Gage ignored her. If she wanted a Pepsi so bad, she'd take her ass in the store and get it herself. He was tired of being nice.

He reached under his seat, searching with his hand until he felt the handle of his .357. He peeked in the rearview mirror to make sure Hakim couldn't see him, then pulled the gun out and tucked it into his waistband.

Arrissa sucked her teeth. "See, that's why we need to move. If you feel you need that just to walk a few feet to a damn gas station, something ain't right."

Gage had his hand on the door handle, about to get out but

stopped. He looked over at his wife. A look of disgust was on her face.

"It ain't even that deep," Gage said. "And we are moving. I agreed to buy that expensive ass house you like. You ain't satisfied yet?"

"Well, leave it in the car if it ain't that deep," Arrissa said.

"Leave what in the car?" Hakim leaned between the driver and passenger seats.

"Sit your little ass down." Gage didn't mean to be so stern, but his frustration level was bordering murderous.

Hakim quickly sat back in his seat.

Gage locked eyes with Arrissa. "That's what you want? You want me to put it the fuck up?"

"Yep," Arrissa said, without blinking.

Gage pulled the gun from his waistband and stuffed it back under the seat. "You happy now?"

"Why thank you, dear." Arrissa's voice was dripping with sarcasm.

Gage got out of the car, slamming the door shut behind him. A few minutes ago he didn't want to drop Arrissa off, now he couldn't wait to get rid of her. She was pushing every last one of his buttons.

As Gage walked into the store, another man was walking out. He felt he knew the man from somewhere but couldn't place him.

"My bad, homie," the man said, smiling, killing the tension. He walked over to a black Bonneville that was parked directly in front of the store and got in.

Relaxing a bit, Gage approached the store's counter. He and the Arab clerk exchanged salaams then he paid for forty dollars' worth of gas and grabbed a couple of Snickers bars for Hakim.

Gage walked out of the store, his eyes on the empty parking space the Bonneville left behind. The gears in his head were still turning, trying to put a name or at least a place with the man he bumped into. He couldn't stand when he didn't remember someone. With all the dirt he did over the years that wasn't a good thing. Mistakes like that got people killed every day.

WHEN IT HITS THE FAN

When he got to the rear of the Infinity he was surprised the gas tank's door was already open. Arrissa finally did something useful. He twisted the gas cap off, then removed the nozzle from the pump and stuck it into the gas tank's portal. He locked the nozzle's handle in place so that the gas could pump itself while he watched his surroundings.

Nothing was out of place but something did catch his attention. He spotted a dude he was locked up with named Paul, selling books on the outskirts of the gas station.

Gage headed in Paul's direction. It was only right he supported the man's hustle. He remembered Paul always talking about selling books and owning his own bookstore.

"Oh snap," Paul said as Gage approached, "they finally let you out, huh?"

"Yeah, man, I beat them on appeal." Gage slapped hands with Paul then pulled him in for a hug.

"That's what's up. So what are you doing now, staying out of trouble?"

"Trying to, but you know sometimes that shit manages to find you."

"I hear that. You gotta keep it pushing though. Ain't no sense getting caught up in the bullshit.'

Paul didn't say anything wrong, but Gage wasn't up for a lecture on how to live right.

"Let me get all three parts of The Tommy Good Story," Gage said, pointing to a line of books that were written by Leondrei Prince, an author that repped Gage's hometown of Wilmington. He read the books already; they were good too, so the ones he bought now would begin his personal library. "Let me get that new Al-Sadiq Banks joint too."

Paul put the books into an all-black plastic bag then handed the bag to Gage.

"How much?" Gage pulled out his wallet from his back pocket.

"Forty dollars," Paul said.

"I know you gotta be killing them, selling the books cheap like that." Every novel Gage bought while he was locked up cost him

153

fifteen dollars plus shipping.

"It's a grind out here. It's hard competing with all the bookstores. Dropping the price makes it a little easier."

"You keep the prices low like that you'll corner the market eventually. You already scored a customer with me." Gage passed Paul a fifty and told him to keep the change.

"That's good looking out, dawg." Paul hugged Gage again.

"Make sure you spread the word for me."

"I got you."

Gage was halfway to the Infinity when the Bonneville pulled back into the Getty's parking lot and came to an abrupt stop in front of him. The tinted passenger's window slid down. The man he had bumped into pointed a black, semi-automatic handgun at him.

Gage remembered exactly who the man was now. It was the same dude with the scar on his face that he and Esco shot it out with outside the bar. He reached in his waistband. Shit, no gun. He was caught naked

The blast from the gun was deafening.

The first shot slammed into Gage's chest, spinning him around. More bullets drilled into his right side and arm. He fell face first to the pavement, his body feeling as if it was on fire.

Tires screeched across the parking lot.

The Bonneville was gone.

Gage tried to move but couldn't. He was tired. Sleepy. His eyes closed. He struggled to open them again.

He had to fight.

His family needed him.

He stared at the back of Arrissa's Infinity. How could he die in front of his wife and son?

WHEN IT HITS THE FAN

Chapter Thirty seven

"I'm about to say fuck this war you got going on with them Delaware niggas," Bone said. "I don't see how I let you talk me into coming down to this deathtrap ass house anyway."

"See that's the problem." Flip knocked the ashes from his blunt onto the carpeted floor. "You young niggas don't know shit about war."

Bone looked over at Newz who was seated on the couch next to him. They both wore the same sly grin on their faces. Flip had to be joking. The mushroom cloud of wet smoke that hovered over his head clearly screamed he didn't know much about war himself. What type of "War General" would voluntarily move to the city of the people he was beefing with and not have enough common sense to stay sober?

"I know enough to know that nigga Esco would've died today," Bone said.

"I'm with Bone on this one," Newz said. "We could've got them niggas today."

"Y'all don't think they was ready for that?" Flip looked at Newz then locked eyes with Bone. "They probably had a whole squad of niggas waiting for us to show up to that funeral. I don't know how many times I got to tell y'all this, but I'ma say it again- I've been doing this shit for years. While y'all was riding big wheels up and down the block, I was knocking niggas heads off."

Bone let out a sigh of frustration.

"All that huff'n and puff'n ain't gonna change shit." Flip stood up, taking a pull from his blunt. "You little niggas just need to listen sometimes. I'm about to slide to the store. Y'all want something?"

Bone shook his head no.

"I'm straight," Newz said.

Flip picked up a forty cal. that was on the coffee table and tucked it in his waistband. "I'll be back in a few," he said, heading to the front door.

The moment Flip slammed the front door shut, Bone looked over at Newz. "Fuck what that nigga talking about. We need to handle them niggas and get this beef shit over with. We ain't even getting money like that right now cause of this shit."

"I feel you on that, but we at least need a plan or something."

"I got a plan. I was gonna say something to Flip, but fuck that nigga right now. He ain't even thinking clear, so he ain't gonna agree with nothing nobody else say anyway."

"What you got in mind?"

"My home girl Jamie put me on to some shit," Bone said, leaning back on the couch with a confident swag. "She said Esco and that bitch suppose to be getting married in a couple of weeks."

"So you want to shoot the wedding up?" Newz asked with a raised eyebrow.

"You mutha fucking right. I'm trying to get this shit over with ASAP. And what's quicker than killing them both at the same time?"

Newz looked as if he was thinking things over.

"What's there to think about?" Bone asked. "We gonna have the drop on them. Is you with me or what?"

"Fuck it, I'm with it. But I think we should run it by Flip first."

"Fuck Flip. We gonna handle this situation, start making money again and if he don't get it together, we gonna do our own thing. I ain't let'n that nigga hold me back no more."

WHEN IT HITS THE FAN

chapter
Twenty eight

Detective Johnson stormed into Christiana Hospital determined to get some type of lead. He flashed his badge at the woman that sat behind the information desk and demanded Gage's room number. When she informed him that the patient he wanted was in ICU and suggested he come back in a few days, he almost snapped.

Maybe it was the liquor? Maybe it was the mounting pressure from the case he was working? Whatever it was, his ability to accept the word "no" was nonexistent. He threatened the woman with charges of hindering a homicide investigation and was quickly given the information he needed.

On the elevator ride up to Gage's room, Detective Johnson thought over the things he would say. He was sure his run-in wouldn't be with Gage, a plus he desperately needed. He knew for a fact that son of a bitch wouldn't help him even from his deathbed. Mrs. Parker, however, was a totally different story. If he played his cards right she'd be begging to tell him any and everything she knew.

When the bell chimed and the elevator doors slid open, Johnson strolled out already knowing where he was going. He'd been on the ICU floor at Christiana Hospital more times than he could remember.

As expected, a uniformed officer was seated on an uncomfortable looking chair, in front of Gage's room. Johnson flashed his badge then walked past the officer without saying a word.

WASIIM

Mrs. Parker was seated at her husband's bedside when he walked into the room. Her back was to him, but he could tell she was crying.

"I need to have a word with you." Detective Johnson's tone was harsh.

Arrissa turned around, her head covered with a scarf, tears in her eyes, but still surprisingly beautiful. She scowled when she saw the detective then rolled her eyes and turned her attention back to Gage.

Detective Johnson felt like he was living in a mob flick. Even the women had problems talking to the police.

"Mrs. Parker, it would be in your best interest if you talk to me about what's going on here."

She didn't respond.

Detective Johnson's patience was running thin. "Regardless if you talk to me or not, I know what's going on, so I'ma tell you. Your husband came home from jail and started a bunch of shit that's claiming lives. Innocent lives. It won't be long until it's you lying in a hospital bed. But then again, you'll probably end up like Sharron and get killed over this shit."

Mrs. Parker stood to her feet, and faced him. The icy glare in her eyes didn't chill the detective one bit.

"You have some nerve," Arrissa said her voice low and even, "To come in here, while my husband is barely clinging to his life, accusing him of crimes when he is the victim. What's your name so I can call your supervisor and tell him about this."

"Detective I-don't-buy-your-bullshit. I don't believe for one second your husband is some innocent victim. And if he lives, he's going to wish he died because I'm going to send him to jail for the rest of his fucking life."

"Get out," Arrissa screamed. She walked over to the detective and shoved him. "Get out now."

Arrissa swung at the detective, her fist coming inches to his face before he grabbed her by her wrist. "Calm down before I charge you with assault."

She snatched away from him but kept her gaze locked with his.

WHEN IT HITS THE FAN

Johnson pulled out one of his business cards. "If, and I do mean if, your husband is an innocent victim, I suggest you clear his name. He's going to be facing a lot of time behind bars. More than likely the rest of his life. If you love him, you'll spare him and yourself the pain of him going back to jail by helping me with my investigation. You said he's innocent." He extended the card to Arrissa. "Prove it."

chapter Thirty nine

Two days passed and Gage was still in a coma.

Arrissa was stressed.

She watched doctor after doctor come in and poke at her husband. They constantly checked this and that, but no one could, or they just wouldn't, answer the one question she wanted to know: was her husband going to live?

It's too early to tell, and *pray on it*, were the only two phrases the doctors said in English. Everything else that came out of their mouths was a bunch of medical bullshit she didn't understand.

Detective Johnson harassing her about helping with his investigation only added to the king size headache she had. It was bad enough he came by the day before, smelling like a liquor factory, but to be so rude and try to blame everything on Gage was crossing the line. Sure Gage played a part in what was going on, but the truth would always remain the same.

Everything was Esco's fault.

Esco set Flip up to be robbed.

And Esco wouldn't give up that troublemaking bitch of his.

Arrissa flirted with the idea of telling Detective Johnson the little she knew. It wasn't fair for her family to suffer for Esco's mistakes. The only thing that stopped her from picking up the phone was Gage. She knew he hated rats and prided himself for being one of the few men that still stuck to the street code. Even though she'd be the one snitching, she knew her working with the detective would reflect on Gage negatively, especially since there was a new wave of rats that used women to do their dirty work so their names wouldn't pop-up on anyone's paperwork.

Arrissa heard the door to Gage's room swing open and turned around to see who was coming in. Her blood pressure rose at the sight of Esco. She jumped to her feet.

"Why the fuck are you showing up two days after the fact?" She said, taking a few steps towards Esco.

Esco looked taken aback by her words.

"Don't look at me like that." She pointed her finger at Esco. "It's your fault my husband is laid up in that bed, and you're just now showing up to check on him."

"I just found out what happened not even an hour ago. I shot straight up here to see what's up. And as far as this shit being my fault, I don't even know what's going on."

Arrissa sucked her teeth. "You're a fucking liar. This whole situation is your fault. If you didn't send those bitches to rob Flip my husband wouldn't have got shot."

Esco's jaw almost hit the floor.

Arrissa felt triumphant like a cat that cornered a mouse.

"I hate you," she spat. "First I get kidnapped because of you, now my husband is in ICU, and you want to sit there like you don't have a clue to what's going on. I wish they would've killed that bitch at her doctor's office."

"Watch your fucking mouth." Esco took a step towards Arrissa.

She took a step back, afraid Esco was going to hit her.

"That bitch you talking about is my fiancée, and she carrying my seed. I'm telling you, if I ain't fuck with Gage the way I do, I'd smack the shit out of you. You better learn to watch your fucking mouth. You don't know what you're getting yourself into fucking with me."

A vicious dog now cornered the triumphant cat. Esco's glare and twisted facial expression spoke nothing but murder. In another setting Arrissa was sure things wouldn't have went in her favor. She decided to keep quiet before her tongue wrote a check her ass couldn't cash. She was hoping she hadn't said too much already.

Esco took a deep breath. "You know what, I'ma do you a favor and leave. Make sure you let Gage know I came by to check on him."

Arrissa let out a sigh of relief when Esco finally left the room. She didn't realize how afraid she was until she noticed how badly her hands were trembling and how hard her heart pounded in her chest. She sat back down in her seat, staring at her husband. She had no intentions on telling him about Esco's visit. If she mentioned Esco to anyone, it would be Detective Johnson.

WHEN IT HITS THE FAN

chapter
Forty

Gage woke up starving. He looked around, took in the fact he was in the hospital hooked up to all types of machines, but focused on the Burger King bag sitting on a rolling tray next to his bed. Arrissa sat on a chair next to the tray, her face in a book.

"What's in that Burger King bag, babe?" Gage asked.

Arrissa dropped her book. The biggest smile Gage had ever seen stretched across her face. "Baby, you're up," Arrissa said. "Alhamdulillah!"

Arrissa sat on the bed with Gage and showered him with kisses. He savored the moment, pleased that his wife was happy. When she finally calmed down, he questioned her about the Burger King bag again.

"Now that's just greedy," Arrissa said, beaming. "You finally wake up after what, four days, and all you can think about is food. You do remember you were shot, don't you?"

Not only did Gage remember he was gunned down at the gas station, he remembered who did it too. He was pissed just thinking about the situation, not so much at the shooter, but at himself for not being on point. He should've recognized the man from the big ass scar he had on his face when he first walked past him.

"If you ain't eat in four days, you'd be hungry too, now give me that bag, woman."

"Boy, you're so silly. Ain't nothing in there. That's what I had for lunch. Besides I have to speak with the doctor first to see if it's even cool for you to eat right now. I'm sure they're going to want to take a look at you."

"Alright, so you gonna handle that now?"

"Yes, baby. I'm at your beck and call."

"And I'm at yours." Gage stared at his wife and could see the stress in her eyes. Guilt tugged at his heart. He was sure her stress was a direct result of the things he'd been doing.

"Everything's gonna be cool, baby. I promise," Gage said as Arrissa stood from the bed.

She bent down and kissed him on the lips. "Insha Allah."

"Hey, baby, where's Hakim?"

"With your mom. They were out here earlier. I'll call after I speak with the doctor. I'm sure she'll come straight here." Arrissa then turned and left the room.

Gage was glad to know his mom had been to see him. Their relationship hadn't been the same since his brother was murdered. He often wondered if she knew he played Cain to his brother's Abel.

He shook the sudden thoughts of his brother Breeze from his mind then closed his eyes and pondered his next move. He needed to get out of the hospital as soon as possible. There was no way he'd stay there longer than he had to. He hated hospitals. He also needed to speak to Esco to let him know what really happened. It was an easy guess to say that everyone probably thought Flip was behind his shooting.

Gage's eyes shot open at the sound of steady clicks coming from the hallway. He recognized that sound anywhere. It was the melody of a woman strutting in a pair of heels. When the clicks were in his room, he tenderly turned his body towards the door and was shocked by who he saw.

Erica approached his bed, a shy smile curled the corners of her lips. She looked nervous and should've been. Despite how good she looked with her hair down and her curvy body stretching the fabric of her clothes to the max, he wasn't happy to see her.

"Anthony, before you kick me out, please listen for a minute. I promise this won't take long."

Gage said nothing; he just stared at her.

WHEN IT HITS THE FAN

She took a deep breath. "I'm sooo sorry I didn't believe you, Anthony. But you have to at least try to understand how things looked. I mean, they did find all that stuff in your apartment. How could anybody not think it wasn't yours?"

"What everybody else thought didn't matter. What mattered was you didn't believe me after I told you that shit wasn't mine. Why couldn't my word have been enough?"

"I don't know, Anthony. I was confused. Scared."

"Scared? I was the one facing all that time in prison, not you. So how the fuck was you scared?"

"I told you my friend was killed behind dating a drug dealer. I didn't want that to happen to me."

Gage recalled the story Erica told him about her friend. She was shot in the head while someone was trying to kill her boyfriend. The story didn't resemble her and Erica's situation even a little bit.

"That ain't got nothing to do with us. You was supposed to stick by me."

"I know and I'm sorry I didn't." A tear slowly trailed down to Erica's chin before falling on her shirt.

"Is that all you have to say?"

Erica wiped her face. "I never stopped loving you."

"Then you shouldn't have left him," Arrissa said, standing in the doorway.

Gage looked around Erica and watched Arrissa storm in. The two women locked eyes. Gage hoped they didn't fight even though he wouldn't have mind seeing Erica get her ass whipped. He just didn't want his wife to get locked up for doing it.

"Who are you?" Erica asked.

Arrissa stuck her chest out like a proud peacock. "His wife."

Erica's pecan complexion paled then reddened.

"Now if you would," Arrissa said, "please excuse yourself so I can tend to my husband."

Erica looked as if she was going to throw up. Gage almost felt sorry for her. He watched as she scooted out of the room with her head hung low. She looked back at him once more then she walked out of the room.

WASIIM

"The doctor will be here soon," Arrissa said, as if Erica was never there. She sat on the bed next to Gage. "When he's done, do you want me to get you something from the cafeteria, or do you want me to ask your mom to bring you something up?"

"Both."

"Greedy." Arrissa laughed, then kissed Gage on his forehead.

"I love you."

"I love you too."

chapter
Forty one

"This is your last night as a free man," Beefy said. He stood on top of the couch that was in the middle of the room and stretched his arms out. "You got this plush ass suite in the Sheraton. It's supposed to be a rack of butt naked bitches in here."

Esco, sitting on a recliner positioned next to a large window that gave view to Wilmington's downtown area, stared at Beefy. He was annoyed that his friend was still ranting about a damn bachelor party.

"I already told you," Esco said. "I got other shit on my mind right now."

Beefy jumped down from the couch. "And some strippers will be happy to erase those thoughts."

"I'm good." Esco directed his attention to the window. The night's sky was clear. No clouds. No stars. The moon, half-full, lay lazily against an inky darkness, looking happy to be alone.

"I hear that," Beefy said. "I'm about to shoot to the liquor store before it close. You want something while I'm out?"

"Naw, I'm straight," Esco said, still staring out the window.

"I'ma holla at you in a few. Hopefully you'll be in a better mood when I get back."

The room's door opened then slammed shut. That was music to Esco's ears. He was thrilled to get rid of Beefy, even if it was only for a few minutes. Any other time Beefy's presence would be more than welcomed, but tonight Esco needed to figure some things out. The wedding he was having tomorrow was only part of his worries. It was the conversation he had with Gage days ago that wasn't sitting right with him.

"Flip didn't shoot me," Gage had said.

That statement changed everything.

Esco thought about how he wanted to handle the situation. Deep down inside he wished Gage had never gotten involved with all the shit he and Sinnamon had going on. He couldn't understand why the man didn't just walk away from the drama when he had the chance to. It wasn't like anybody was putting pressure on him. He himself had told Gage to chill. The dumb ass nigga had a family. The more Esco thought about things, the more compassion and respect he lost for Gage. That made his decision a lot easier. If Gage didn't care about his own family, why should he care about them.

He heard the room door open then ease shut. If that was Beefy, he didn't come back alone. Esco couldn't see the door or the immediate area around it from where he was seated, but he could tell at least four or five people were in the room. Naturally he reached for his pistol, a titanium .357.

Music suddenly blasted throughout the room. It only took a second for Esco to recognize his own voice on the track. He relaxed and listened.

Dance with a general, party with a gangsta/Concord boys get cute too but we so dangerous/the weed like glue boo bud stay stinking/loose off that Grey Goose her ass keep shakin'/that's just the usual short on the basics/tell em what we use to, GO HEAD, GET NAKED!

Three thong-wearing women, built like stallions, trotted into the room followed by Beefy, Reef, and Clark. Beefy's smile showed every last one of his teeth. Esco couldn't have kept himself from grinning even if he wanted to. Not only were the women looking good dancing to his music, but Clark, who wasn't even home a whole week from the hospital, was walking under his own power.

Clark, holding two bottles of Ace of Spade in the air, rapped the words to Esco's song louder than the music itself. He poured the champagne all over the women.

"You heard what the song said," Clark shouted. "Get naked!"

The party was officially started.

chapter
Forty Two

"I'm checking out today," Gage said, sitting on the side of his hospital bed. He wasn't feeling one hundred percent but felt good enough to get the hell out of the hospital.

"No, you're not." Arrissa stood in front of him with her arms folded across her chest, a defiant look on her face. "The doctor said you should stay for at least another week."

"And I said I wasn't staying here longer than I had to. You heard what the man told me yesterday. I'm fine, I don't have to stay."

"But he also said you should stay longer."

"Should and have to are two different things. Would you want to be stuck in here if you didn't have to be?"

"I'ma do whatever I feel is best for my body. Why are you in such a rush to leave today anyway?" Arrissa put her hands on her hips and leered at Gage. "I know you don't think we're going to Esco's wedding."

Arrissa's whole demeanor pissed Gage off. He understood her worries and all, but she crossed the line thinking she could dictate his moves. Gage stood to his feet. Arrissa seemed to shrink right before his eyes. She recoiled as if he was going to hit her, an insult in his eyes. As much as he wanted to lately, he wouldn't put his hands on her. She was his wife.

Gage spoke stern but as gently as he could. "You need to learn to trust me."

"I do trust you. It's your friends I don't trust. There's just too much going on, and every time I turn around you're finding a way to run back into the middle of things."

"Going to a wedding ain't getting into the middle of nothing. It's only a wedding."

"A wedding we don't need to be attending. We're *supposed* to be separating ourselves from them. You promised we would."

"And I'ma keep that promise. We're going to move to Florida in that nice house you want, and we're going to live like royalty like we supposed too."

Arrissa looked at Gage with sad eyes. "Not if you keep jeopardizing this family."

"I'm not jeopardizing this family."

"Really, Mujahid? You sure you're not just trying to protect your reputation?"

Arrissa's words stung. How could she even think he'd put his reputation over his family? What type of man did she think he was?

"Is that what you think this is all about, my fucking reputation?"

"Sometimes I don't know what to think. You're a liar. I swear, some days I wish I had it in me to hate you, so I could walk away."

"I never lied to you."

"You did. You talked about change so much while you were in jail. How no one or anything could draw you back to the streets." Streams of tears flowed from Arrissa's eyes. "Babe, you just don't know. Sometimes when I lay alone in that bed at my grandmother's house, knowing I should be laying next to you, I wish you were still in jail, *talking* about your dreams. At least then I could still have hope...I use to dream about you coming home just about every night; Us having more kids, living the American dream but still being good Muslims. Laa ilaha illallah, Muhammad-ur-Rasul-Allah. You said it and I said it, Mujahid. We can't keep turning our backs on this deen. If you're going to stand up for anything, it should be Islam. I understand some of our friends may have been killed, but that doesn't give you the right to shed someone's blood, especially the blood of another Muslim. You're wrong, Mujahid, and you know it."

WHEN IT HITS THE FAN

Arrissa's sharp words cut Gage so deeply he sat back down on the bed. He leaned forward, resting his elbows on his knees. He felt like a hypocrite. He taught Arrissa everything she knew about Islam, yet she had to reiterate the basics to him just to get his attention.

"How many blessings of your Lord will you deny?" Arrissa said.

WASIIM

chapter
Forty Three

The pearl white and blue carriage came to a stop at a royal blue velour rug that stretched across the field to the pavilion Esco and the Pastor stood under. Rows of people were seated on each side of the rug, creating the aisle Sinnamon would soon be walking down. The crowd craned their necks in the direction of the carriage. Through a small window, Sinnamon stared back at them with a smile on her face.

Betty had outdone herself. The décor was more beautiful than Sinnamon had pictured it would be. She couldn't imagine how her mother pulled things together in such little time, but her fairytale was coming true right before her eyes.

The driver of the carriage opened the door and let Shaquan out. He looked like a little man dressed in his tux. Sinnamon smiled at him and he smiled back, extending his hand to her. She let him help her out of the carriage. The moment her heels touched the rug the guest let out an array of "awww's."

A pianist began to play the traditional "Here Comes the Bride" melody. The guest stood to their feet. All eyes were on Sinnamon. Even the sun seemed to smile down on her, its rays planting soft kisses on her slender shoulders. Everything was perfect. She began her walk to the man she'd be spending the rest of her life with.

As she walked down the aisle, Sinnamon zeroed in on her teary eyed mother. Betty stood at her place as the Matron of Honor, not typical for a mother, but that's how Sinnamon wanted things to be. She couldn't think of a better woman for the job.

172

WHEN IT HITS THE FAN

When Sinnamon and Shaquan reached the Pastor and Esco, Shaquan presented his sister, then took his spot with the rest of the groomsmen.

Sinnamon stood face to face with the love of her life, crying behind her veil as he promised to love her through thick and thin, for better or worse, until death do them apart.

She promised the same.

After the couple exchanged vows, the pastor said, "You may now kiss the bride."

Esco lifted Sinnamon's veil.

What sounded like cracks of thunder interrupted the moment.

The guests let out screams of terror.

Something was terribly wrong.

Esco knocked Sinnamon to the ground. She looked up in time to see two masked gunman about fifty yards away sprinting in their direction, bright flashes of fire breathing out the barrels of their guns.

Esco pulled a handgun from the inside of his suit jacket and returned fire. The gun blasts exploded in Sinnamon's ears, leaving them ringing. She clamped her hands tightly over the sides of her head and prayed that the two men would turn and leave, but they didn't. They continued to charge forward, hurling bullets in her and Esco's direction.

Esco dropped to his knees, clutching his shoulder. A crimson blotch grew where the bullet struck. One of the groomsmen pulled him to his feet and tried to lead him away from the mayhem, but he jerked from the man's grasp and ran back over to her. He snatched her by her arm, dragged her to a safe spot behind the pavilion, then ran back into the chaos, his gun kicking like a wild bull with each shot fired.

One of the gunmen finally dropped, grabbing at his stomach. The other one tried to help him, but fell himself. He got back up, fired a few times then tried to help his partner again. He managed to lift the man to his knees, but that's as far as he would make it. Bullets tore into the wounded man's back. He fell to a heap, hopefully dead. The last gunman sprinted to a late model van, got in and sped off.

The gunfire finally stopped.

Sinnamon wiped the tears from her eyes and took a few deep breaths in an attempt to calm down. Her body was shaking. She needed to get herself together.

She looked out into the crowd. Flipped over chairs and frightened looking people were everywhere. Some peeked from their hiding places not sure if the coast was clear. A little boy ran to a man and hugged him. That's when Sinnamon realized Shaquan wasn't by her side.

"Shaquan!" she yelled.

She ran out into the crowd, searching for her brother. Her heart galloped in her chest. She pushed people out of her way as she looked around.

She spotted Betty's shoes. She'd recognize them anywhere. She ran over to where her mother was crumpled on the ground. Betty's dress looked as if the top part of it had been painted burgundy.

"Mom," Sinnamon whispered, kneeling down next to her mother. She lifted Betty's head. It was wet with blood. What she saw next caused her world to stop.

Underneath Betty, Shaquan lay motionless, his eyes glazed over. A dime size hole was in his forehead. The only family Sinnamon had was dead.

And it was all her fault.

Suddenly her breathing shortened. She became lightheaded and felt nauseous. She blinked once and everything went blurry. When she blinked a second time everything went black.

chapter
Forty Four

"I fucked up, Flip," Bone yelled, walking into the house. "I fucked up."

"What the fuck is you talking about?" Flip asked, from his seat in his La-Z Boy recliner. He looked Bone up and down and noticed his head was wrapped in a bloody tee shirt. "What the fuck happened to you?"

"Newz is dead."

Bone's words knocked the high out of Flip. For the first time in days he began to think with a clear mind. "What the fuck you say?"

"Them niggas killed Newz."

"What happened?" Flip said as calm as he could. He stood up and walked over to Bone.

"I don't know what went wrong. We went to handle Esco for you—"

"Handle Esco? I ain't tell you niggas to make a move, so what the fuck is you talking about, Bone?"

"We had the drop on him and his bitch. They got married today."

Flip rubbed his hands over his head then took a deep breath. "Let me guess, you niggas thought it'd be a good idea to shoot the wedding up?"

Bone dropped his gaze to the floor.

"Who idea was it?" Flip asked even though he knew the answer. Only Bone would make such a bold move without checking with him.

Bone sat down on the couch and hunched over. It looked like he might've been crying, but Flip couldn't tell and didn't care. One of the most thorough young boys he ever had on his team was dead, and it was Bone's fault.

"Answer me, nigga. Who came up with the bright fucking idea to shoot up the wedding?"

Bone glared at Flip like it was his fault Newz was dead. "What difference do it make? Pointing fingers ain't gonna bring him back."

"It make all the difference in the world, Bone. I know it was your dumb ass idea. It had to be. You need to listen sometimes. I told you before, you don't know every fucking thing."

"I ain't trying to hear that shit right now." Tears flooded Bone's face. "That was my best friend. You can try and blame me all you want, but at the end of the day this shit is still your fault. This your beef, and it should've been handled. If you wasn't getting high every five minutes, shit wouldn't be like this."

Flip inched closer to the .45 that was lying on the table next to his La-Z Boy. Killing Bone was the only logical plan he could come up with. One, no, two shots to the head, and like magic, another problem would disappear. But he couldn't do it in the house. A proper investigation, some pressure on the woman whose name the house was in, and the police would have him as a suspect.

"Go home," Flip said.

Bone jumped to his feet. "I ain't going home until we handle them niggas."

"I'll handle the shit myself. Police probably looking for you. Eventually they gonna know Newz was from Philly. Damn, shit about to get hot."

"Fuck that. We need to handle them niggas now."

"Listen." In three long strides Flip was breathing down Bone's neck. "We walking on thin ice right now, especially you, so fall back. Go home and stay the fuck out the way."

Bone took a step back. "Niggas ride out for you at the drop of a dime. Newz is dead, now you talking this fall back shit. Mutha-fucka it's been hot. I'ma do shit my way from here on out. I don't need a sucka nigga like you around."

It took every disciplined fiber in Flip's body for him to let Bone walk out of the house. That pussy deserved to be dragged out in a black bag. He couldn't wait to catch him in the streets.

chapter
Forty Five

"How is she?" Esco asked the nurse that was tending to Sinnamon. They were in the emergency section of Christiana Hospital in one of the small rooms.

"She's fine. The doctor gave her a sedative so she could relax and get a little rest. You'll be able to take her home in a few hours."

"What about the baby?"

The nurse smiled widely. "Your baby's perfect. Just make sure your wife takes it easy when she gets home. And you make sure you keep that wound of yours clean. I'll give you a sling and some bandages before you leave."

When the nurse left out of the room, Esco grabbed a hold of Sinnamon's hand and kissed it softly. Looking at her sleep in the hospital bed made him think back to when she'd been shot. That thought, and the fact her mother and brother were dead, made him question his ability to protect her. He felt he was doing a poor job.

That had to change.

Esco's cell phone buzzed in his pocket. He fished it out and looked at the caller ID. Reef was calling.

"What's up?" Esco answered.

"I think I got a line on them Philly niggas," Reef said. "When you think you gonna be able to holler at me?"

Next to finding out he was going to be a father, that was the best news Esco ever heard in his life. He wanted to get with Reef right then, but knew he couldn't. "I'ma get at you as soon as I get my wife straight. That's gonna be a couple hours though. That cool, or do we need to jump on this now?"

"Ain't no rush. It's best we wait 'til tonight anyway. Just holler at me when you ready."

"Alright, I'ma get with you in a few." Esco disconnected the call then sat back down in his chair hoping everything would come together. After a while he figured he'd pay Gage a visit since he was already at the hospital and had nothing better to do.

Gage was seated upright in his bed when Esco walked in his room. Esco slapped hands with him, then plopped down on an empty chair beside the bed. He noticed two stuffed duffle bags laying awkwardly on another chair and said, "You finally packing up I see."

"Yeah, I can't wait to get out of here," Gage said. "What's up with you though, I thought you was getting married today? What happened to your arm?"

Esco leaned towards Gage and whispered, "Them niggas shot my wedding up. I only got grazed in my shoulder, but Sinnamon's mom and brother got killed. A few other people too. Shit got messy."

"Damn, that's fucked up. How's your wife and the baby?"

Esco studied Gage's face for a split second. He seemed sincere.

"They cool," Esco said. "She's downstairs right now, but look, I ain't come to holler at you about that."

A look of concern crossed Gage's face. "What's up?"

"I might got a line on Flip and them. I ain't one hundred percent sure yet, but I'ma find out later. You want me to let you know if everything's a go?"

Arrissa ease dropped from the bathroom, straining to hear what Esco's trifling ass was telling her husband. She knew he came to bring bad news the moment she saw him stroll in with his arm in a sling. That's why she stayed in the bathroom. She didn't catch everything Esco said but understood clearly when he said he had a line on Flip. She prayed Gage would say he didn't want anything to do with what Esco had going on.

WASIIM

"Hit me up as soon as you know what's good," Gage said a little too eagerly.

Arrissa burst out of the bathroom with the intent to scream and curse at Gage until her face turned blue. Then it hit her, an answer to every last single one of her problems. She calmed down, grabbed one of the duffle bags she packed, then faced her husband. "I'm going to start taking things down to the car," she said in the most pleasant voice she could muster.

"Alright," Gage said. He was so wrapped up in what Esco was saying, he didn't offer to help her with the bags or suggest she get one of the orderlies to do it. To say she was pissed was an understatement, but still she smirked, pleased with the plan she had. With the duffle bag strapped over her shoulder, she slid out of the room with one thing on her mind.

chapter
Forty six

"So what's the look?" Esco asked, sliding into the passenger seat of Reef's Lincoln. They were parked on the side strip of Concord Avenue, right up the street from the barbershop. Reef was laid back in the driver's seat puffing on a strong smelling blunt of weed. The smoke fogged the car up pretty good. Esco just hoped it didn't fog Reef's memory. He needed to know every detail possible.

Reef snubbed his blunt out in the ashtray of the door panel. "I was coming out my homegirl's spot where I told you I was gonna take the hammers after that shit popped off at the wedding. So I'm on the porch and I hear this loud bang. I look across the street and see a nigga coming out a house."

"Where the bang come from?"

"I guess the nigga slammed the door or something. He looked pissed. His head was wrapped in a bloody tee shirt or something, so I figured he must've been fighting with his bitch. You know how that go."

"So what, you recognized him or something?" Esco asked.

"Naw, I don't think I ever saw him before."

"So how you figure he linked to Flip?"

"I don't know why, but I watched the nigga for a minute. He got into a van that looked just like the one at the wedding. Same color, same make. And the mutha-fucka had PA tags. I sat out there for a minute trying to see if anybody else came through there or left, but the spot was dead. That's when I called you."

WASIIM

Esco soaked in the information. It wasn't much, but at least it was something to go on. He figured if that house was where Flip and his little crew were hiding they'd be long gone by now.

"How you want to handle it?" Reef asked.

"I want you to run me past there real quick. I want to see if there are any cars on the block with PA tags."

"Then what?"

"Regardless of anything, I'm in there. By myself though. This something I gotta take care of on my own time."

"You sure?"

"Positive. If I need you, I'll let you know."

"If that's how you want it." Reef started the car then put it in drive. "We'll shoot through there now."

chapter
forty seven

Sinnamon laid curled up in the middle of her bed, her mind a projector for the worst moments of her life. She had to be one of God's rejects, better yet, Satan's beloved. That could be the only explanation as to why so much blood was on her hands.

She squeezed her eyes shut as tight as she could in an attempt to swallow herself in complete darkness. That didn't work. Images of her dead loved ones plagued every space in her mind. Essence, Mrs. Jones, Betty and Shaquan, each of them flashed into her memory, bloody and dead, seemingly taunting her with glazed over eyes.

"I can't live like this." She screamed loud enough to make the words scratch her throat.

She dragged herself out of her bed and began to pace her room. Normally, the way the plush carpet hugged her feet brought her a little comfort at least, but now each step she took reminded her of how deep she was sinking into hell.

With that thought, she darted down the stairs and ran straight to the kitchen cabinet where Esco normally stored his alcohol. Unfortunately, when she swung the cabinet doors open, the only thing that stared back at her was the pipe connected to the sink's drain.

"Shit."

She slammed the cabinet doors shut. She should've known Esco had gotten rid of all the liquor in the house. The coke too. That didn't stop her from looking though. It took her more than an hour to search every spot she could think of. As expected, she came up empty handed.

Sinnamon stormed up the stairs and back into her bedroom. She found a rubber band on her vanity tray and used it to pull her hair back into a long ponytail. It was time to hit the streets. She jumped into a pair of flats then tossed on a light jacket. She grabbed her purse and keys on her way out the door.

Driving was irritating. The Chrysler 300 she had as a rental was an insult. It drove nothing like her Bentley. All that money she paid for insurance, she should've been given a rental that was the same quality as her car or better. If she didn't get some coke soon, she was going to flip out. Everything was starting to annoy her.

Before she realized it she was on the west side of Wilmington. She hadn't a clue on where to go to get some coke, but she was sure she could find it on the west side. The area was flooded with drug activity. Her biggest concern was whether or not the coke would be as good as the batch she skimmed from Esco. She highly doubted it, but it didn't matter. As long as she was able to get high and escape her reality, quality meant absolutely nothing.

She cruised past the corner of Fifth and Franklin where a pack of young boys were posted. They looked like hustlers to her. She sped up a bit and parked her car around the corner. She snatched a pair of Ray Bans from her visor, put them on, then took a look in the visor's mirror. The sunglasses alone weren't a very good disguise. She needed something else. A scarf would've been perfect, but she didn't have one. At least in that car she didn't. She flipped up the hood to her jacket and studied herself in the mirror again. She looked more like a movie star trying to go incognito than a drug addict, but the look suited its purpose. No one would be able to tell Esco they saw her on a street corner buying drugs.

She took three crisp one hundred dollar bills from her purse and slipped them into her jacket pocket, then got out of the car. Quick and simple she told herself. She practiced what she'd say to the dealers as she walked.

She settled on telling them that she had $300 and leaving it at that. They could take it from there.

WHEN IT HITS THE FAN

"Damn, look at her, she phat as a mutha-fucka," one of the hustlers said, as she approached. All eyes were on her after the rude compliment. She stood there trying to force the correct words from her mouth.

"You lost or something?" A baby-faced hustler said, taking a step in her direction. He couldn't have been more than fifteen-years old.

"I—I got three hundred dollars," Sinnamon said.

The way all of the hustlers gawked made her feel uncomfortable and dumb.

"You get high?" The little boy asked.

"I got three hundred dollars," Sinnamon said. The crowd of hustlers chuckled.

"I got her," the one who made the rude compliment said. He stepped towards Sinnamon with his hand stretched out. "Give me the money."

Sinnamon did as she was told.

The man dipped into the alleyway and returned about a minute later.

"One time, one time," one of the hustlers yelled.

The man that had taken Sinnamon's money pushed a package in her hand, then walked off with the rest of the crowd.

Sinnamon saw a police cruiser ride slowly down the block. Her heart galloped in her chest. How could she explain going to jail? She stuffed the package in her panties as discreetly as possible then walked up the street. She wanted to run so bad her legs trembled.

The cops rode past her. They didn't even look in her direction. She let out a gush of air then hurried to her car.

Behind the wheel of the car, she finally felt safe. She pulled the package out and sat it on her lap. The familiar light blue, wax coated bags made her shiver.

Heroin.

What was she going to do with all those bags of dope. She wanted to run around the corner and mash the package in the hustler's face for insulting her. The memory of the cops stalking the area quickly nixed that idea. She peeled a single bag from one of the rubber-banded bundles. "Golden Peace" was stamped on it.

The word peace leaped out at her. She recalled the blissful expression on Betty's face every time she used the drug. Betty didn't seem to have a care in the world when she was high. Sinnamon wanted that for herself. She wanted to be numb and not care about anything but wasn't sure if she could stomach using heroin.

"I'll never be like Betty," she mumbled.

She looked down at the bag again. The word peace smiled up at her. One time wouldn't hurt she decided. She was mentally stronger than Betty.

There was no way she'd get addicted. It wasn't like she had plans on ever using it again after today. Tomorrow she'd be back to normal. Esco wouldn't even be able to tell. Peace would be hers for this one night.

chapter Forty eight

"Come on in, Mrs. Parker," Detective Johnson said, opening the door for Gage's wife. "Have a seat." He shut the door then sat be- hind his desk concentrating on how not to make himself look like a complete idiot. When Mrs. Parker called and said she had some information for him, he literally did a cartwheel. Now that she was right there is his office, it took every fiber in his body for him not to jump on her like an oversized dog and lick her face.

Mrs. Parker eased into the seat on the opposite side of the desk, her face stern, almost angry. He wondered if her mood had any-thing to do with the all black garbs she wore. A woman as beauti-ful as she was had to hate covering herself up like that.

"How can I help you?" Johnson asked. A smile tugged at the corners of his mouth but he was able to suppress it.

Mrs. Parker took a deep breath then began her story. She con-firmed that all the murders were related and that everything was Sinnamon's and Esco's fault. She told him about Flip but couldn't give him Flip's real name; she didn't know it. He believed her too. He believed everything she said until she swore that her husband was totally innocent in all that was going on. He almost laughed at that one. Innocent people don't get intertwined in multiple murders.

"I think they're all going to meet up soon," she said.

"Who?"

"Esco and all his friends. Probably my husband too."

"Do you have an idea when?"

"No, I'm not really sure."

"Where are they going to meet?"

"They normally meet up at the barbershop. At least that's where my husband always goes when he has to talk with Esco. I don't see why things would change."

Detective Johnson could go with that. When he went in the barbershop in hopes of getting a lead on his partner's death, it looked as if he interrupted a meeting.

"And you think they're going to go after this Flip guy?"

"Wouldn't you if you knew where he was and he was trying to kill you?"

"Are you sure?"

"Look, Detective, I already told you I'm not one-hundred percent sure about anything. I'm only able to tell you the little bit my husband told me and about the things I was able to piece together on my own. I heard Esco with my own ears say that he had a line on Flip. It doesn't take a rocket scientist to figure out his next move."

"Okay, I'ma look into it."

"That's all?" Arrissa frowned. "What about my husband?"

"You coming here today may have saved him from a lengthy prison sentence. I'ma keep an eye on Esco and the barbershop. You just make sure you keep your husband away from his friends for a while. Once the cuffs begin to snap shut, you don't want your husband around."

"But what if his name comes up, or I can't keep him away?"

His ass is going to jail. "I'ma do whatever I can to help him. His best bet would be to help himself."

"He's not going to do that."

"Mrs. Parker, how about we cross that bridge when we get there?"

"No, how about we cross it now. I didn't give you that information for your benefit alone. I gave it to you so you could help my husband."

"I understand that, Mrs. Parker, but there's only so much I can do. If your husband gets tangled into all of this, I'm not sure I'll be able to help, and that's just me being real with you. You'd have to get him to cooperate. Only other thing that might help, and I stress the word might, is if you testify. The info you've given me so far means nothing unless you're willing to take the stand." Johnson leaned closer to her. "Are you willing to take it that far?"

Mrs. Parker didn't say anything for a minute. Detective Johnson prayed she'd say yes. If she did, he'd see to it personally that Gage was arrested.

"For my family," Mrs. Parker said, staring into Detective Johnson's eyes. "I'm willing to do whatever it takes."

After Mrs. Parker left, Detective Johnson tried to figure out a game plan. He paced his office as he thought. His biggest obstacle would be to convince his supervisor, Dan, to give him proper back up. The information Mrs. Parker gave him was nothing more than a good tip. She wasn't a witness to any of the murders. Everything she said was speculation. Believable, but still speculation. His boss was a stickler for hard facts, so the likelihood of him agreeing to send an all-out blitz of detectives and S.W.A.T. officers directly at Esco, the way Detective Johnson wanted, was slim. He needed something more concrete.

There was a loud knock on his
door. "Come in," Johnson shouted.

The door popped open and his boss wobbled in. *Speaking of the devil*. May as well plead his case now instead of later.

"Boss—

Dan raised a palm, halting him. "Sit down for a second," he said. "We need to talk."

Dan's voice was mournful, so was the look on his face. This had to be bad news. Johnson took his seat at his desk. Dan remained standing.

"Detective, I'ma get straight to the point. You're suspended with pay until further notice."

Johnson jumped to his feet. "No! I finally got a break in my case. You can't do this to me now."

"I didn't do anything to you. You did it to yourself. I told you more than once about your drinking, but you didn't listen. You don't even try to hide it." Dan leaned towards Johnson and sniffed. "You smell like liquor now, for Christ's sake."

"Boss, just listen to me for a minute."

"There's nothing to listen to, Chuck. My supervisors are breathing down my throat because of you. There was nothing I could do. I'm sorry. Just be happy you're still going to get a paycheck."

"What about my case? My lead?"

"The whole department is on it. Your loss was ours you know that. Give me the details of this lead you have, and I'll pass the information to the proper person."

Johnson repeated what Mrs. Parker told him.

Dan frowned. "That's not enough for an arrest, but your informant will be perfect for trial. We'll keep contact with her and see if we can get anything else before we make a move."

"That's it?" Johnson shook his head in disbelief.

Dan put a firm hand on Johnson's shoulder. "I'm sorry about this, Detective, but it wasn't my decision. Get a hold of your drinking while you're off, get a fresh start when you come back."

"How long am I suspended?"

"I can't say. You have to get counseling and attend a few AA meetings. Hopefully, it won't be long."

There was an awkward pause.

"I need your gun and your badge," Dan said in a low tone.

Johnson dug his police wallet from his pocket and gave it to Dan.

"Gun."

Johnson opened the top drawer of his desk and grabbed his gun. He popped the clip out then handed both the gun and clip to Dan.

"I'll be in touch," Dan said, then walked out of the office.

"Fuck," Johnson yelled. He grabbed a hold of his desk, flipped it over, then crumpled to the floor and sobbed. Once again, he failed his partner.

chapter

Fortynine

Sinnamon slammed her bathroom door shut and locked it. If Esco came home he wasn't going to bust in on her this time. She sat on the toilet, then removed a compact mirror, a credit card, a dollar bill, and one of the bundles from her purse. She peeled a bag from the bundle, tore the bag open with her teeth and dumped the heroin onto the mirror. The little bit of powder that spread across the glass surface couldn't possibly ease her pain the way she needed it to. She ripped two more bags open and dumped them out onto the mirror, then used the credit card to arrange the powder into a neat line. The thought of ripping another bag open crossed her mind, but she decided against it.

She rolled the dollar bill into a tight straw, and used it to snort the heroin. Her body relaxed instantly. She laid back against the toilet tank and bathed in a sensational feeling of peace. Her heartbeat slowed to a steady beat. Euphoric was the only word that could describe how she felt. Her worries were no longer cement shoes sinking her to the bottom in an ocean of misery.

Just as fast as the peace came it vanished. Chaos replaced it. Before she could stop it, vomit flew out of her mouth and onto her lap.

Her heartbeat slowed more. She broke into a cold sweat.

She tried to stand but her body refused to cooperate. The room began to spin. Black spots floated in front of her eyes. She tried to shake the feeling but couldn't. The last thing Sinnamon remembered was her face slamming into the tile floor.

WASIIM

chapter
FIFTY

Esco eased into his driveway, parked next to Sinnamon's rental, then slipped out of his car feeling a little upbeat. The trip over to the house Reef told him about was a good move. Not only was there a car sporting PA tags parked about a block away from the house, but he was able to get a good feel of the surrounding area. His plan was coming together well. He knew exactly how he was going to get into the house and had three good escape routes.

The moment he walked through his front door an eerie feeling gripped his chest. The house was too quiet. He leaped up the stairs, his gun leading the way. He stepped into his bedroom.

Sinnamon wasn't there.

He scanned the room for any signs of a struggle. There were none. He relaxed a moment. If he wasn't sure about anything else, he was sure that Sinnamon wouldn't have allowed herself to be taken without a fight.

He spotted a yellow glow of light shining from the bottom of the bathroom door. His first thought was Sinnamon was in the bathroom getting high. He tried the knob but the bathroom was locked.

"Open the fucking door," he yelled, banging on the door with the butt of his gun.

Sinnamon didn't respond.

"Bitch, I said open the fucking door."

Esco kicked the door as hard as he could. It flew open and banged against the wall. He spotted Sinnamon laid out on the floor.

WHEN IT HITS THE FAN

The crotch of her light colored jeans was crimson. He knelt beside her and used his index and middle fingers to feel around her neck until he found a faint pulse. She was still alive. He prayed the same was true for his child.

He hoisted her over his shoulder and noticed three empty dope bags on the floor. He couldn't believe his wife had stooped so low. If she wasn't pregnant he would've left her in the bathroom to die.

"HELP! HELP! I think my wife overdosed," Esco yelled, bursting into the Wilmington Hospital Emergency Room. "She's pregnant." A team of nurses ran over to Sinnamon and put her on a gurney.

They pushed her through a set of double doors as they worked on her. Esco tried to follow but was stopped by another nurse who wanted some information about what was going on. He told her what he knew, then was forced to sit in the waiting room where surprisingly only a few people waited.

He glanced up at the clock that hung on the wall in front of him. It read 6:09. He could hear every second that ticked by. One-thousand, two hundred thirty-seven seconds later, a doctor wearing a lab coat and hospital scrubs walked into the waiting room. He spotted Esco and walked over to him.

"You can see your wife now," the doctor said.

Esco had no desire to see Sinnamon. Besides Flip, he couldn't think of anybody he hated more than her at that moment. Her stupidity was probably going to cause their baby to have brain damage or worse.

"How's the baby?"

The doctor grimaced. "I'm sorry," he said. "The baby didn't make it."

"When will my wife be allowed to go home?"

"We'll monitor her for the night. She can leave in the morning." Esco took a deep breath then stood to his feet. His legs trembled beneath him. Tears welled in his eyes but he refused to let them fall. He walked away from the doctor and out of the hospital with murder on his mind.

chapter
FiFTy one

"I'm out after tonight," Esco said to Beefy. The two men were seated in Esco's car in front of Beefy's house.

"Out as in leaving Delaware," Beefy said, "or out like you leaving the game."

"Both."

Beefy smiled. "I dig that. I'ma do the same eventually. Where you and the wife moving?"

"The wife ain't coming. That's what I needed to holler at you about."

Beefy looked sincerely sad. "Yo, man, I'm sorry about how things turned out at the wedding. I thought we'd had everything under control before it got that messy."

"It ain't ya fault, homie, don't even trip. I need you to handle something for me though."

"What's that?"

Esco looked Beefy square in his eye. "Sinnamon gotta go," he said.

"Huh?"

"I don't have time to explain right now. I got to catch up with my white boy to get a few things I need for my move, but I want that bitch gone. You think you can handle that for me?"

"If you're sure then I got you," Beefy said.

"Man, I ain't never been this sure in my life. I would do it myself but I don't got the time to handle that and everything else I need to handle."

"Say no more. I got you."

Esco dug in his pocket and pulled out his cellphone. "Everything is erased out this joint except my connect's number," he said, handing beefy the phone. "In exactly a week I want you to call him. He'll be waiting to hear from you. Once y'all set up a meeting, toss this joint."

"Alright, cool," Beefy said, shoving the phone in his pocket.

"Where you want me to catch Sinnamon at?"

Esco pulled a piece of paper from the driver's side visor. "This the address to the crib. She'll be there tomorrow. Burn the whole house down with her in it."

chapter FIFTY TWO

Overdosing taught Sinnamon two things. One, three bags of good dope at one time was too much for a new comer, and two, Esco's love wasn't as true as she thought it was. Okay, she lost the baby, that was her fault, but did he have to leave her at the hospital alone without hearing her side of the story? Didn't he just promise to love her for better or worse, through thick and thin? If that was the case, why wasn't he there with her or at the hospital last night? Or even there in the morning when she was released. She almost died. He didn't even call to check on her. No one did.

She hated life. Suicide danced in her mind more than once. She was a hair away from slitting her wrist when she walked into her house that morning. The only thing that stopped her was Lady Heroin. The bundles she brought yesterday were still on the bathroom floor. She tried to flush them down the toilet but couldn't. The peace she felt that split second before everything went bad wouldn't let her. She needed to feel like that again so she sniffed a bag. The world was a better place after that. Every time her high went down she vacuumed another bag up her nose. At the rate she was going, every bag would be gone in a week or so.

She needed money.

She searched the house from top to bottom and only found a thousand dollars. Esco, that petty bastard must've took all the money with him. He must have taken his guns and jewelry too because none of that was in the house either. He was lucky because if she found anything valuable, she would've sold it just to be spiteful. It wasn't like she really needed his money. She had plenty locked away in a few safety deposit boxes. Speaking of which, it was time she went and got her money and found another place to stay. She was probably risking her life sleeping in Esco's house. He did say he'd kill her if she lost the baby. She took a quick shower, then dressed in a simple pair of jeans, a cotton long sleeved shirt and a comfortable pair of flats. She grabbed her and Esscence's safety deposit box keys from their hiding space under the carpet in Shaquan's room and stuffed them in her purse.

Before she left, she put her car keys, the money she found, and a steak knife in her purse just in case she happened to run into any unwanted company. Mainly Esco.

chapter
fifty three

Gage stared at the number that flashed across the screen of his vibrating cell phone. The number was new to him. He was tempted to answer, but instead, he sent the call to his voicemail, and laid the phone down beside him on his bed. The person's number wasn't programmed in his phone, so they couldn't have been important. If there were some type of emergency, the caller would do the ob-vious and leave a message.

He pushed the unknown caller out of his mind and focused his thoughts on his wife. He couldn't wait until she got out of the shower. She owed him a night to remember after all of the time she spent at her grandmother's house. He was surprised she agreed to stay home with him now. In fact, she agreed so fast he thought she was up to something. It wasn't until after she told him that Hakim was staying with her grandmother for a few days that he relaxed.

Gage's phone vibrated again. This time he had a text message.

Get at me ASAP, it's ya boy, the text read. It was sent from the same unknown number that had just called him. Something was up. Against his better judgment, Gage called the number back.

"Who playing on my phone?" Gage asked, when a male voice answered.

"Relax, nigga, ain't nobody playing on ya phone."

Gage recognized Esco's voice and sat up. "What you got a new phone or something?" Gage asked.

WHEN IT HITS THE FAN

"Yeah," Esco said. "I lost the other one."

"I hear that. What's up though? Tell me something good."

"Everything looking beautiful on my end. You remember what I told you at the hospital right?"

Gage smiled. "That's a go?"

"It's a go," Esco said. "I need you on this one too. You know I wouldn't even ask you if I didn't need you. You think you healthy enough to ride with me?"

"I'ma little sore but I can move around pretty good. When you trying to head out?"

"Meet me up the way in a half hour."

"Shit," Gage mumbled under his breath. He wasn't sure how he was going to pull this one off. Arrissa would probably try to fight him if she caught him trying to leave the house. The shower water was still running so he would have to be quick.

"I'ma throw my shit on now," Gage said. "Don't leave me."

"I got you," Esco said.

Gage hung up the phone. He dressed in a pair of black cargo pants, Timberlands and a black hoody. The shower water was still running by the time he was done.

"Babe, I be right back," he said, standing in front of the bathroom door.

"What the hell you mean you'll be right back? Where are you going?"

"I need to run to the store real quick."

Arrissa knew Gage was lying the moment the words rolled off his tongue. "Hold on a minute. Let me rinse off. I'm going with you."

"Take ya time, babe. I'll be back before you're done."

Arrissa heard Gage stomp down the steps. She had to stop him. If he was planning to meet Esco both of their lives would never be the same. She wasn't sure if their marriage would last if she were forced to testify once Gage got himself locked up. He wouldn't understand she was doing it for him...for their family.

She jumped out of the shower dripping wet, then darted out of the bathroom. She bounced down the stairs stark naked. The roar of Gage's engine was like a punch to her stomach. By the time she made it to the front door Gage's taillights were fleeing down the block.

"Damn it." Arrissa slammed the front door shut. There was only one option left. She leaped up the stair,s three at a time and burst into the bedroom. She dialed Gage's cell number from her cell phone as she dressed in a pair of sweat pants and a tee shirt. There was no time to put on her garbs. She was running down the stairs with her car keys in her hand by the time Gage's voicemail picked up. She ended the call and shoved the phone in her pocket. If she broke every traffic law known to man, she'd have a good shot at catching Gage before he made it to the highway. If she had to ram her car into his to stop him, then that's what she was going to do. Whatever it took, she was going to save her husband.

She swung the front door open and stopped in her tracks. There in front of her stood a man wearing a black ski-mask. The man pointed a revolver in her face. She took a step back. Then as if in slow motion, she watched as he pulled the trigger. The first shot felt like it caved her chest in. She fell to the floor and could feel blood filling her lungs. She tried to crawl away but the man kicked her in her side. Blood flew from her mouth as a gush of air escaped her lungs.

The kick hurt just as bad as the gun shot. The man kicked her onto her back and stood over her, gun in hand. She looked into his eyes and knew she was about to die. She squeezed her eyes shut, bracing herself for the pain.

Four more shots echoed before her world went black.

WHEN IT HITS THE FAN

chapter
fifty four

It was dark when Sinnamon made it back home. She lugged two rolling suitcases into the living room, then plopped down on the couch. Things didn't go exactly as she planned. She wasn't given access to either of Essence's boxes even though she had the keys. That was stupid. If she had the keys then obviously she had permission to get into the damn boxes. At least she was able to get her own money without any problems. Almost a million dollars in cash. Robbery had been good to her. If push came to shove, she might have to revive her career as a robber. For now, the money she had was more than enough to keep her comfortable until she figured out what she was going to do.

That was a good question. Getting high was at the forefront of her plans at the moment, but that was temporary. The life of a junkie wasn't an option. She only needed to use drugs for a little while longer. She wasn't ready to face the world sober. The moment she got her emotions in check, she'd quit dope cold turkey. That couldn't be too much harder than quitting coke.

She pulled herself from the couch and made her way up the stairs. Her day had been long. She needed to do a bag to really relax, so she locked herself in her bathroom where she felt a sense of privacy. She'd never get high out in the open, even if she was in the house.

She heard the sound of glass shattering in her bedroom. Esco had to be back. Why didn't she leave when she had the chance? She sniffed a bag in case he busted in on her and took her supply.

201

WASIIM

If she had to face him, it was best to do it high. She'd be able to absorb his verbal and physical abuse easier that way.

More glass shattered.

What the hell was he breaking? Sinnamon composed herself, then stuffed all the dope she had left into her purse. If she had to make an escape there was no way she was leaving a single bag behind. She took a quick inventory of her purse.

Dope? Check.

Car keys and knife? Check, check.

She had everything she needed. She strapped her purse over her shoulder then took out her knife and gripped the handle tight. She'd stab Esco if he got carried away. And why wouldn't she? It wasn't like he loved her.

She stepped out of the bathroom and walked into an inferno. She took a step backwards. Fire and smoke almost consumed her entire bedroom.

She tucked the knife back into her purse, then crawled out of her bedroom on her hands and knees. She had to make it downstairs to her money.

The hallway was fire free but the smoke was thick. She crawled to the staircase and looked down. The first floor was swallowed by flames. Every dime she had robbed and killed for was gone.

Another glass shattered.

Someone was firebombing the house. She crawled into Shaquan's room. A small fire was beginning to spread on the carpet. She crawled her way to a window on the far side of the room. It was broken. She knocked the shattered pieces of glass out of the frame with her purse, and jumped.

She hit the grass hard. The impact jarred her legs, and it felt like she broke one of her ankles. Through the dark, she spotted a black figure jump over the fence in her backyard and run away. She wished she had a gun because if she did, she would've shot whoever it was in the back.

She stood up, adjusted her purse on her shoulder, and limped around the house to her driveway. Her car sat perfectly fine in the same spot she parked it. A crowd of noisy neighbors had formed a

WHEN IT HITS THE FAN

semicircle around her house and was staring at the fire. An older white woman asked her if she was okay, but she ignored the woman and got into her car, slamming the door shut behind her.

Of course, she wasn't okay. What type of moronic question was that? Her fucking house was on fire along with almost a million in cash.

She started her car, put the gear in reverse, and mashed down on the gas pedal. Her tires squealed and the car launched backwards. A few of her neighbors had to jump out of the way. She made a k-turn when she hit the street and raced away from her misery.

chapter FIFTY Five

Detective Johnson watched the barbershop through a pair of night vision binoculars he "borrowed" from the special unit at the police station. He was in his car, parked a few blocks from the barbershop, waiting patiently for Esco to show his face. Being fired, or suspended with pay as Dan put it, wasn't going to stop him from acting off of the tip Mrs. Parker gave him. On or off the force, he was going to take down his partner's killer if that was the last thing he did.

A car stopped in front of the barbershop then parked. Johnson was surprised but more than happy when Gage got out of it. Mrs. Parker must've had a harder time keeping an eye on her husband than she anticipated. Gage's arrest and her testimony would easily be the nail in the coffin for his partner's killer; would probably earn him some type of medal as well. The least it would do was get him his job back. He took a swig of gin straight out of the bottle, thinking how tonight was the night.

A few minutes later another car stopped in front of the barbershop. Gage got into the passenger seat. Johnson zoomed in on the driver. It was Esco.

"Bingo," Johnson said, dropping the binoculars on his lap. He started his car and shoved the gear into drive. Esco's blinker signaled he was turning right onto Washington Street.

Johnson sped down the street, then turned onto Concord Avenue. and barreled towards Washington. Esco cruised past right in front of him when he was forced to stop at the light. He waited fifteen seconds before he ran the light and turned onto Washington. Esco and Gage seemed to be headed to the west side.

"Where the nigga at?" Gage asked, slipping on a pair of baseball gloves.

"Over there on Linden Street," Esco said.

"How we gonna do this?"

"I'ma kick the door in, and we gonna run up in there like it's a robbery. Ain't nothing special to this shit."

"You got a strap for me, right?"

"You already know."

Esco pulled a .357 revolver from underneath his thigh and passed it to Gage.

The rest of the ride was silent. Esco kept his eyes on the road as he went over his plan again and again. It was almost like he was alone. He didn't think about Gage again until he parked the raggedy car they were in.

"The spot right around the corner," Esco said, opening his car door.

Gage followed him to the house Reef pointed out earlier. Through the windows, the house was dark except for the familiar flashes of a TV. Somebody was home. The car with the PA tags was still in the same spot. Hopefully, Flip was the only one in the house.

Esco stepped quietly onto the porch. Gage was right on his heels. Esco gave the door one kick and it flew open. They ran into the house with their guns drawn.

They found Flip seated on a La-Z Boy recliner in the front room. A big cloud of smoke hovered over top of his head and all around him.

Esco didn't have the least bit trouble recognizing the smell of PCP. He stared at Flip. The man was wetted out of his mind. His eyes were glazed over and he didn't move an inch. He just stared out into space. He was gone. Perfect. Gage moved quickly to the other side of the room and peeked his head in the kitchen.

"Ain't nobody else in here."

Esco drew another gun from his waistband and aimed it at

Gage's head. "Why the fuck you cross me?"

Gage's eyes grew so wide they could've fallen out of their sockets. He returned the favor and pointed his gun at Esco.

"What the fuck type time you on, Es?"

"Don't act surprised, nigga. I got this shit figured out. Ya dumb ass wife slipped up and told me she got kidnapped. You ain't tell me that one, so I put two and two together. You the only one I told about Sinnamon's doctor's appointment. You gave Flip the line on me to save your bitch. You was going to let that nigga kill my seed."

Gage pulled his trigger.

The gun clicked. Metal against metal. He pulled the trigger again with the same result.

"I gave ya wife all five of them," Esco said, then squeezed the trigger to his nine. A bullet exploded into Gage's forehead, sending Gage to the floor with a thud.

Esco focused his attention and aimed both guns at Flip. The mutha-fucka still didn't move.

"Drop your weapon now," a deep voice called out from behind him.

Esco froze. Only the police spoke like that. He craned his head to the side but was sure not to point either gun in the direction of the cop. He spotted Detective Johnson, alone, aiming a .40 cal. at him. He knew he had a chance to make it out of the situation alive and free if he played his cards right.

"So you gonna let this nigga get away with killing ya partner," Esco said, knowing he'd strike a nerve.

Detective Johnson eyed Flip.

Esco did the same.

Flip didn't move an inch. If his chest weren't heaving up and down, Esco would've thought he was dead.

"That's right, that's the mutha-fucka that killed your partner right there. If you're going to arrest me, let me kill him first, or at least let me watch you kill him. I see you ain't got no back up. So you got to be on this on your own. Nobody will ever know."

Sweat glistened on the detective's forehead and the side of his face. The desire to kill was etched in his eyes.

"Come on, you might as well kill him. You know you want to. Your partner would want you to. I'll never say a word. I just want to see this nigga die as much as you do."

Detective Johnson's gun flared and echoed throughout the house. Flips head snapped back. Blood leaked from a small hole in his face. The detective looked drunk with satisfaction.

Esco didn't waste a second. He fired two shots. One slammed into the detective's head and the other tore into his throat. The detective crumpled to the floor. Esco walked over to him to make sure he was dead.

He was.

The detective wasn't part of Esco's plan, so he had to improvise. He tucked his unused gun back into his waistband, then put the gun he killed the detective and Gage with in Flip's right hand. He made sure Flip's finger was on the trigger. How the media reported the scene was beyond his control, but he knew the police wouldn't be fooled. With another one of their own dead, the streets were definitely going to feel the heat. If the FEDS weren't involved yet, there was no doubt in his mind that they would be involved now. He was getting the fuck out of the country.

Tonight.

THE END

So Real You Feel You've Lived It!

A SHORT TREAT FROM A FUTURE AUTHOR

ENJOY!

WHEN IT HITS THE FAN

DUMBBELL
By
Donnell Kurtis

Saturday afternoon, I was in the living room of my third floor apartment, doing dumbbell curls, and listening to the new Felon's Quest song that blared from my stereo's speakers when my front door flew open and Mr. Eakin — my five-foot-four, Napoleon-complexed landlord – barged in. He leered at me with those googly little fish eyes of his, then slammed the door closed, stalked over to my stereo, and yanked the cord from the socket.

I dropped the ten pound dumbbell I was curling on the rug and jumped to my feet.

"Are you crazy, old man," I said.

Eakin marched right over to me. We stood eye to eye as he tried his best to intimidate me with his glare. His scowl deepened however, when he figured out I wasn't the type of woman that was going to back down.

"Dubeck," he said, calling me by my last name. "This ain't no homeless shelter. I need my rent money."

He got no argument from me. I needed this apartment, and I only had enough money to pay half the rent I owed. I wiped my hands on the bottom of my gray wife beater, grabbed the small roll of bills I had for him from the coffee table, handed them to him, and then brushed past him on my way to the stereo.

"What kind of shit is this?" he asked.

I didn't respond so obviously, he'd count the money. I bent down and picked up the stereo's cord from the floor.

"Where's the rest of my money, Dubeck?"

I pretended to have trouble getting the plug back in the socket, hoping he'd just blow off some steam complaining and give me until my next payday to settle my debt.

Eakin apparently had something else in mind, because next thing I knew, the pervert was behind me grabbing me by my waist and grinding himself against my ass. "Don't worry yourself," he said. "We'll work something out."

My fighting instincts immediately took over. I spun around, pushed him off of me and launched a left hook to his jaw.

He stumbled back two steps. His eyes crossed, his mouth went slack and he swayed on his feet. Then, as if in slow motion, he crumpled to the floor, his head landing right on my abandoned dumbbell.

I didn't panic. Maybe this wasn't as bad as it looked. I walked to the kitchen and filled the mayonnaise jar I use for drinking with water from the tap, went back to the living room, stood over Eakin — who was still out cold — and threw the water in his face.

He didn't budge.

I leaned over him to get a closer look. He wasn't moving. No rise and fall of the chest, no nothing. This couldn't be happening. I grabbed him by the shoulder, ready to shake him back to life if I had to. That's when I noticed the blood seeping from the back of his head onto the rug.

At that point a normal person probably would have called an ambulance, but I wasn't normal by a long shot. I'd just finished a three year bid for running my ex-boyfriend over with a car. I was on parole, and a dead man in my living room definitely wasn't going to score me any points with my parole officer, especially when the dead man also happened to be my landlord. So I did what any ex-con in my position would do-started thinking of a way to get rid of the body.

First, I needed to get him out of my apartment. I moved everything off the rug; the secondhand sofa, the coffee table, my dumbbells, workout bench, and the empty pizza box from last night's dinner – everything but Eakin. The rug, I'd been told, was an imitation Persian left by the previous occupants when they moved out. It was a little worn around the edges but definitely large enough to wrap Eakin in. I got down on my knees to check Eakin's pockets, but before I could get started, someone knocked on my door.

WHEN IT HITS THE FAN

I froze. Wasn't expecting company. Didn't know who it could be.

"Who is it?" I yelled.

"Ms. Fennelly," came the reply. "Here for a random home inspection, Ms. Dubeck."

Oh shit. Marya Fennelly, my parole officer. "One minute," I called back. I quickly rolled Eakin in the rug, dragged the rug across the room and leaned it in the far corner by the window. Then sweating and breathing hard as if I'd just run a marathon, I opened the door.

Dressed in a dark women's pant suit and a pair of cheap black loafers, Ms. Fennelly stood in my doorway with her arms folded tightly beneath her too large breasts. "What took you so long, Ms. Dubeck?"

I threw a glance over my shoulder at my workout bench, which was pushed over near the stereo. "I was in the middle of a workout. Why didn't you let me know you were coming; I'd have straightened up a bit." I flashed her a smile, which she duly ignored before stepping past me into the apartment.

"If you had known I was coming," she said, "there would have been no point in doing a random check now would it?" She then started her inspection. In my small one bedroom apartment that amounted to no more than opening and closing a few drawers and closets. In about five minutes she was done and on her way out.

After she left I waited a few minutes. Then I opened the front door and peeked into the hallway. Seeing no one, I dragged the rug out into the hallway and penned it against the wall with my shoulder while I locked up.

No sooner than my key turned the lock, my next door neighbor Todd exited his apartment with his pitbull Misty in tow.

The dog barked. Maybe at me, maybe at the rug, I wasn't sure which, but it was at that moment I lost my grip on the rug, and it tilted over and thumped to the floor.

The pitbull immediately ran over to the rug, sniffing and pawing at the end which had fell near Todd's door. My heart thudded in my chest.

"Get away from there, Misty," Todd said, yanking on the dog's leash. "Sorry about that, Dubeck." He eyed the rug for a moment, and then he looked at me. "You want a hand with this thing?"

"I'm okay. I'm just taking it to the car."

"Well, me and Misty are going for a walk, but I'm sure Misty won't mind if I help a pretty lady out a little."

"That's okay, really, I'm parked right out back in the parking lot."

"Even better. Me and Misty always go out through the back anyway."

I groaned inwardly when Todd reached down to grab hold of the rug. Suddenly, Todd's door opened for a second time, and his girlfriend Cindy appeared in the doorway. Her eyes landed directly on me and of course the sweaty wife beater that was glued to my sports bra. She gave me a look that actually made me shiver, just as quickly the look was gone and replaced by a plastic smile just as Todd looked at her over his shoulder.

"What's up Cin?" Todd said.

"I just wanted to remind you to take out the trash on your way out," she said, flashing another look my way. "Plus I need to talk to you about something before you go anyway— it's important."

Todd looked at me then let the rug go. "Just give me a minute and I'll be right back, Dubeck." I let out the breath I hadn't even known I'd been holding until that moment and said, "Don't worry about it Todd. I'll manage."

Without another word, Cindy took Todd by the arm, led him and the dog back inside the apartment and closed the door.

I knew with Cindy around I didn't have to worry about Todd returning. Still, I needed to get out of the hallway before someone else showed up and decided to help.

I heaved the rug from the floor and started dragging. After four flights of stairs I finally made it to the laundry room in the basement.

The laundry room reeked of marijuana smoke. Three teenage boys, probably kids who lived in the building, sat on the washing machines, smoking and talking. Thankfully, they paid me little attention as I dragged my burden across the basement tiles and out the

WHEN IT HITS THE FAN

back door to the parking lot.

Finally, I got the rug stuffed in the backseat of my old blue Camry. I slammed the back door and ran around to the driver's side all set to get going when I noticed my front tire was flat.

I banged my fist on the top of the car and kicked the tire, ended up stubbing my damn toe in the process too. While I hopped around like an idiot from the pain in my foot, I spotted the solution to my problem at the other end of the parking lot.

Eakin's car.

I wrestled the rug from my backseat, dragged it— limping all the way— to the end of the parking lot and leaned it against the back door of Eakin's Cadillac Seville. That's when I realized my mistake. In my haste to hide Eakin's body when my parole officer showed, I'd forgotten to check his pockets. His car keys were wrapped up in the rug with him.

Suddenly, the back door of the building banged open. The three teens from the laundry room bolted out and ran up the alley. A minute later the old lady who always watched everything from the window of her first floor apartment exited the back door too. She looked up and down the alley before fixing her outraged glare on me.

"Nerve of those kids," she said, "smoking that stuff in my building. I fixed them good though. I called the police." She held up a cell phone and gave a satisfied nod as if she conjured them by her mere mention of them, a police car sped into the alley and pulled into the parking lot.

Two officers jumped out of the car and ran over to the old woman who told them what happened. My heart damn near jumped out of my chest when she pointed in my direction and said, "Ask her. I'm sure she saw which way they ran. She was standing right there when I came out."

One of the officers, the taller of the two, started making his way over to me. "Hey Miss," he said, "let me talk to you for a moment." He sidled up next to me and produced a small notepad from his shirt pocket. "Look, miss, me and my partner just want to put old Mrs. Crane at ease. There's no way we're gonna ride around looking for some kids for smoking pot. So I'm going to act like I'm questioning you , then me and my partner are gonna get in our car and split, and hope that the old woman doesn't call us back out here today about something else as minor as this."

I wiped the sweat from my forehead with the back of my hand and nodded.

"Hey, miss, you don't look so good, you okay?"

Hell no I wasn't okay. My mouth was dry; sweat was running down my face into my eyes; and I kept imagining that at any moment this bumbling idiot with a badge, who couldn't seem to stop looking at my chest, would somehow find out I had my landlord wrapped up in this rug. But what could I do other than keep nodding? That's when the cell phone started ringing. Not mine. I can't afford even a pre-paid one. Apparently, Eakin also had a cell phone on him when I rolled him up.

"You gonna answer that, miss?"

I looked at the officer and flashed a smile. "Probably just my ex-boyfriend calling again."

He looked at me strangely. "I know I'm not crazy," he said, "but it sounds like the ringing is coming from that rug you're holding. What the hell do you got going on here?"

As if in answer to his question, muffled yells started coming from the rug too.

The officer's eye's narrowed. He stepped back, pulled his pistol from its holster and aimed it at me.

"Now, don't do anything crazy, lady. Just step away from the rug and slowly get on the ground."

THE END!.

LOCKED UP BUT NOT
FORGOTTEN

Street Knowledge Publishing LLC
1902-B Maryland Ave
Wilmington, DE 19805
TOLL FREE: **1.888.401.1114**
www.streetknowledgepublishing.com

Date: _____

Purchaser _____

Mailing Address _____

City _____ State _____ Zip Code _____

Qty.	ISB Number	Title of Book	Price Each	Total
	978-0-9822515-6-0	Bloody Money	$15.00	
	978-0-9822515-9-1	Bloody Money 2	$15.00	
	978-0-9799556-4-8	Bloody Money 3	$15.00	
	978-0-9799556-0-0	Tommy Good story	$15.00	
	978-0-9822515-0-8	Tommy Good Story II	$15.00	
	978-0-9746199-1-0	Me & My Girls	$15.00	
	978-0-9746199-0-3	Cash Ave	$15.00	
	978-0-9822515-1-5	Merry F$$kin' Xmas	$15.00	
	978-0-9799556-0-7	A Day After Forever	$15.00	
	978-0-9822515-3-9	A Day After Forever 2	$15.00	
	978-0-9746199-6-5	Don't Mix the Bitter with the Sweet	$15.00	
	978-0-9799556-9-3	Playing For Keeps	$15.00	
	978-0-9799556-3-1	Pain Freak	$15.00	
	978-0-9799556-5-5	Dipped Up	$15.00	
	978-0-9799556-6-2	No Love No Pain	$15.00	
	978-0-9746199-4-1	Dopesick	$15.00	
	978-0-9799556-7-9	Lust, Love & Lies	$15.00	
	978-0-9746199-7-2	The Queen of New York	$15.00	
	978-0-9746199-8-9	Sin 4 Life	$15.00	
	978-0-9822515-4-6	A Little More Sin	$15.00	
	978-0-9746199-5-8	The Hunger	$15.00	
	978-0-9746199-3-4	Money Grip	$15.00	
	978-0-9822515-7-7	Young Rich and Dangerous	$15.00	
	978-1-944151-26-3	Street Victims	$15.00	
	978-1-944151-28-7	Street Victims II	$15.00	
	978-1-944151-30-3	Street Victimes III	$15.00	
	978-1-944151-32-4	A Small Wonder	$15.00	
	978-1-944151-45-4	Coup De Grace	$15.00	
	978-1-944151-47-8	Burton Boys (May 2017)	$15.00	
	978-1-944151-56-0	Burton Boys 2	$15.00	
	978-1-944151-58-4	Burton Boys 3	$15.00	
	978-1-944151-00-3	Dirty Living	$15.00	
	978-1-944151-65-2	Watch What You Say	$15.00	
		Total Books Ordered	Quantity	
			Subtotal	
SHIPPING/HANDLING (Via U.S. Priority Mail) $7.20 for 1st book, $2.00 for each additional book Institutional Check & Money Orders ONLY (No Personal Checks Accepted)			Shipping Total	
		Total	$	

216

WHEN IT HITS THE FAN

Street Knowledge Publishing LLC
1902-B Maryland Ave
Wilmington, DE 19805
TOLL FREE: 1.888.401.1114
www.streetknowledgepublishing.com

Date: _____

Purchaser _____

Mailing Address _____

City _____ State _____ Zip Code _____

Qty.	ISB Number	Title of Book	Author	Price Each	Total
	Butterfly Collection				
		Beautiful Demise	K.D. Harris	$13.99	
		Scarred	K.D. Harris	$13.99	
		Pressure (Coming April 2017)	K.D. Harris	$13.99	
		Dying to Fit In (Coming June 2017)	K.D. Harris	$13.99	
		Legacy (Coming August 2017)	K.D. Harris	$13.99	
		Classy Clique (Coming Sept. 2017)	K.D. Harris	$13.99	
		Caged Secrets (Coming Nov. 2017)	K.D. Harris	$13.99	
		Messy Media (Coming Dec. 2017)	K.D. Harris	$13.99	
	SKP Erotica				
	978-1-944151-04-1	Beyond Measure	K.D. Harris	$15.00	
	978-1-944151-06-5	Beyond Measure II	K.D. Harris	$15.00	
	978-1-944151-62-1	Beyond Measure III (April 2017)	K.D. Harris	$15.00	
	978-1-944151-08-9	The Games We Play	K.D. Harris	$15.00	
	978-1-944151-02-7	For The Love Of It	K.D. Harris	$15.00	
	Eric B Crime Novels				
	978-1-944151-20-1	That Was Dirty	Wasiim	$15.00	
	978-1-944151-22-5	It Gets Dirtier	Wasiim	$15.00	
	978-1-944151-24-9	As Dirty As It Gets	Wasiim	$15.00	
	978-0-9799556-8-6	Money and Murder	Fred Brown	$15.00	
	978-1-944151-35-5	Money and Murder II	Fred Brown	$15.00	
	978-1-944151-39-7	Money and Murder III	Fred Brown	$15.00	
	978-1-944151-49-2	Scandalous Ties	Jermaine "Ski" Buchanan	$15.00	
	978-1-944151-51-5	Scandalous Ties II	Jermaine "Ski" Buchanan	$15.00	
	978-1-944151-52-2	Scandalous Ties III	Jermaine "Ski" Buchanan	$15.00	
	978-1-944151-55-3	Scandalous Ties IV	Jermaine "Ski" Buchanan	$15.00	
	978-0-9799556-2-4	Courts in the Streets	Kevin Bullock	$15.00	
	978-0-9822515-5-3	Courts in the Streets II	Kevin Bullock	$15.00	
	978-1-944151-43-0	Courts in the Streets III	Kevin Bullock	$15.00	
		Total Books Ordered		Quantity	
				Subtotal	
	SHIPPING/HANDLING (Via U.S. Priority Mail) $7.20 for 1st book, $2.00 for each additional book Institutional Check & Money Orders ONLY (No Personal Checks Accepted)			Shipping	
				Total	
		Total		$	

www.ingramcontent.com/pod-product-compliance
Lightning Source LLC
Chambersburg PA
CBHW021618270326
41931CB00008B/750